W9-AUM-171

INSIGHT POCKET GUIDE

RIO DE JANEIRO
AND ITS COAST

Discovery
CHANNEL

APA PUBLICATIONS L
Part of the Langenscheidt Publishing Group

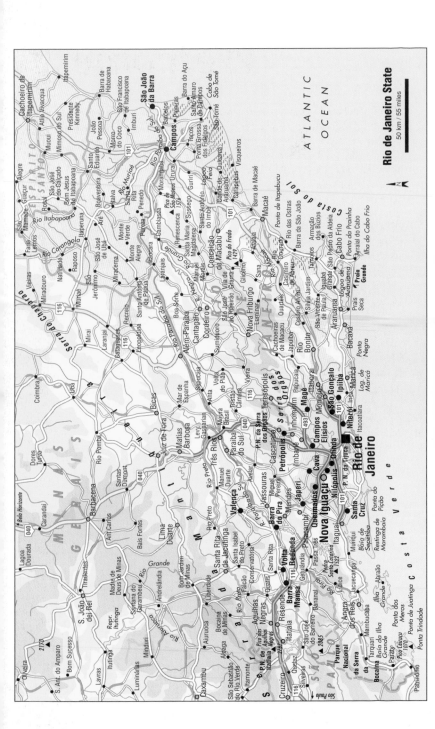

Rio de Janeiro State

50 km / 55 miles

introduction

Welcome

This guidebook combines the interests and enthusiasms of two of the world's best-known information providers: Insight Guides, who have set the standard for visual travel guides since 1970, and Discovery Channel, the world's premier source of non-fiction television programming. Since the hedonistic days of the mid-20th century, when the rich and famous flocked to Rio, and often behaved outrageously, it has been a city with a reputation for pleasure. Things are calmer these days but *cariocas*, as citizens of Rio are called, still know how to enjoy themselves and to welcome visitors. In these pages Insight Guides' correspondent in Rio, Liz Wynne-Jones, has devised a range of itineraries to bring you the best of the city's natural beauties, famous landmarks and historical sights. Five tours concentrate on the city's highlights, while three excursions – inland to an imperial summer retreat, and along the stunning coastline of Rio de Janeiro state, cater to visitors with a little more time.

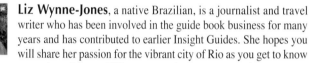

Liz Wynne-Jones, a native Brazilian, is a journalist and travel writer who has been involved in the guide book business for many years and has contributed to earlier Insight Guides. She hopes you will share her passion for the vibrant city of Rio as you get to know its many moods and faces. 'When you pack to go on vacation, put your common sense in the case first,' she says, 'and remember to bring your sense of humor.' Liz is a founding director of the Margaret Mee Foundation, which honors the English painter who fell in love with the natural wonders of Brazil on a visit that was to last a lifetime. The foundation promotes the art of botanical illustration and is engaged in a wide range of conservationist activities.

Pages 2–3: sunset on Ipanema beach
Pages 8–9: young *cariocas* on the beach

Vwattibi

History & Culture

The Portuguese were awarded ownership of the land now called Brazil before it had even been discovered by Europeans. In 1494, six years before the 'discovery,' Spain and Portugal had signed the Treaty of Tordesillas, which carved up the known and unknown world and gave the Portuguese any territory that lay more than 370 leagues west of Cape Verde. The cautious Portuguese did not, at first, take their new land seriously. Explorer Pedro Álvares Cabral landed there by accident, blown off course when sailing to India in 1500. Four years later, Florentine traveler Americo Vespucci stated that 'nothing very useful is to be found on this coast, except for an infinity of brazilwood trees.' He might have been more generous had he realized the value of these trees. They produced brazilin, a much sought-after pigment used to dye cottons, silks, and inks a royal crimson. The dye put Brazil on the world trade map, and gave the country its name. Sadly, it also set a precedent for the devastation of forests, with an estimated 70 million brazilwood trees being felled over the next 300 years.

What is a Brazilian?

The origins of Brazil's indigenous peoples is still punctuated by unanswered questions: no-one is certain where they came from, nor when. It is estimated that there were between two and three million native people in Brazil when the first Europeans arrived. The Rio coast was inhabited by several distinct tribes, of which the Tupinambá were the senior group, numbering some 100,000 people. In 1614, six of them were taken by French Capuchin monks to Paris, where they were the object of great curiosity. South of the Tupinambá lived the Tamoio, true masters of the Bay of Guanabara, who sided with the French and were virtually wiped out in battles for possession of Rio in the mid-1500s. The northern coast of the state of Rio was inhabited by the cannibalistic Goitacá tribe – the ones who caused the Portuguese the most trouble.

At the close of the 20th century, it was estimated that some 700,000 indigenous people have survived, their numbers dramatically reduced by 'flu, measles, and smallpox, not to mention war, persecution, and abysmal living conditions during the time that they were enslaved. They may be fated to extinction: over half the survivors are under 15 years of age, and their life expectancy is a mere 45 years.

The slave trade, initiated in 1533, also made an important contribution to the rich ethnic mix of contemporary Brazil. Slaves were brought to Brazil from virtually every

Left: engraving showing an Indian attack on a Tupinambá tribe
Right: Pedro Álvares Cabral, Portuguese explorer

nation in Africa. One in five did not survive the journey, and those who did lived an average of only seven years. The fact that their ethnic influence is comparatively strong is evidence of the vast numbers brought over from Africa before this trade in human beings was ended in 1850.

The other key ingredient in the racial mix, of course, was provided by the early Portuguese colonists, and those who came in ever-greater numbers after gold was discovered in Minas Gerais in 1693. Far from home, their families a distant memory, they mixed and intermarried with people of all races, colors, and creeds. The children of indigenous women and Portuguese men were known as *mamelucos*; the offspring of indigenous and African couples were *cafusos*; while those born of African–European unions were called *mulatos*. Recent figures indicate that in the Rio area, 62.4 percent of the population considers itself white, 6.6 percent black, 30 percent *mulato*, or somewhere in between, and the tiny remainder a mix of Asian, indigenous, and others.

Religion and Carnival

Organized religion was brought by the Jesuits, who disembarked in Brazil in 1549 with the mission of 'civilizing', educating, and bringing under the inflexible yoke of Catholicism every soul in the land. They encountered much resistance both from the indigenous peoples and the African slaves, who had their own beliefs and rituals. Brazil is, in many ways, a land of compromise and this is nowhere better demonstrated than in terms of religious observance. While nearly 75 percent of the population considers itself Roman Catholic, 20 percent of them also subscribe to spiritualism and non-mainstream religions. African *umbanda* and *candomblé* beliefs co-exist with Catholicism; and the most influential religious current in Brazilian society today is Evangelism, which has brought modern management methods to worship and permeated every level of Brazilian life, especially the political classes.

One religious festival that has shed all vestiges of its solemn origins is Carnival. Once a time of merrymaking in preparation for the lean days of Lent ahead (*carne* = flesh, *vale* = farewell) its religious connotations struggle to be heard over the drum-beats and frenzied singing and dancing that take over the country in the weeks leading up to Ash Wednesday. Rio's first Carnival ball is said to have taken place in the mid-1880s at the Hotel Itália, but street celebrations had been taking place for hundreds of years before that. Slaves and the poorer sections of society made the most of the reigning jollification to dress up in their masters' cast-off clothing and pretend to be gentlefolk. Carnival is celebrated at all levels of Brazilian life, but nowhere quite as madly and lavishly as in Rio, where there are street parties,

Above: a slave trader displays his captives
Right: an *umbanda* ceremony in full swing

impromptu street parades, and elite, glamorous balls in prestigious locations. The public high point of Carnival in Rio is the parade by the premier samba schools, which takes place in the purpose-built Sambadrome, attracting thousands of visitors. Song, dance, costume design, lighting, music, and rhythm, all are on display in what is known as 'the greatest show on earth.'

The First Tourists

Throughout the 18th century, Rio grew rich, as gold from Minas Gerais flowed through its port, and in 1763 it became the official capital. As such, it rose to the challenge of hosting the high-profile visitors who disembarked at Praça Quinze in 1808 – the Portuguese royal family and court, headed by João VI. Fleeing the imminent invasion of their homeland by Napoleon at the start of the Peninsular Wars (1808–14), they decided to take up residence in their tropical colony. The new capital undertook a rapid urbanization program, and Dom João proved to be a good administrator. He established the legal system, the naval academy, a gunpowder factory, the royal print works, Brazil's first newspaper, the botanical gardens, and the Bank of Brazil, and boosted the economy hugely by opening up trade with European countries other than Portugal – a practice that had previously been forbidden.

By 1821 Dom João could no longer ignore the vacancy on the Portuguese throne, nor the spread of republican tendencies in Europe, so he returned home to resume his role, leaving his son, Pedro, in Rio as regent. But this was a turbulent time, in which vociferous nationalists were seeking independence from Portugal. Predictably enough, after much intrigue and political machination, independence was declared the following year, and Pedro became Emperor and Perpetual Defender of Brazil.

Pedro I was not popular, and his blatant legislation in favor of his Portuguese compatriots, at the expense of the interests of native Brazilians, worsened the situation, which boiled over in 1831, forcing the king to abdicate and return to Portugal. His son, also Pedro, was too young to take up the throne, and so a turbulent 10-year regency followed, at the end of which the 15-year-old Pedro was declared king.

The Golden Age of Dom Pedro II

This wise and scholarly ruler, who genuinely loved his country, was able to reconcile the interests of many of his subjects and promote progress. He was aided in this by the fact that the country's economy was boosted by a boom in the coffee trade. An avid international traveler, he brought Rio into the modern world by implementing infrastructure and services that he had seen functioning abroad, such as gas lighting, which first illuminated the city streets in 1854. He also established the practice of retreating from the heat and yellow-fever-bearing mosquitos to the hills outside Rio, and his summer residence in Petrópolis is now one of Brazil's most visited sites.

As time passed, speculation as to who would succeed him increased. His daughter, Isabel, had married a Frenchman, rendering her an unacceptable candidate for the throne. Ironically, it was she who contributed to Pedro's fall; during one of her father's absences abroad, she passed a law that abolished slavery but failed to award compensation to slave owners, who found themselves without a workforce. Dissatisfaction fueled the growing republican sentiments in the country, and in 1889 the monarchy was overthrown in a bloodless coup, a republic declared, and the royals banished to Europe.

The City Comes of Age

The young nation embraced republicanism and the challenges of the 20th century with great enthusiasm. Rio was the capital of innovation and trendsetting, and legislators looked to Europe for models of modernity; 'Paris in the tropics' was the target. Magnificent avenues replaced tenement blocks; entire neighborhoods were demolished to allow fresh air to penetrate the low-lying city center. Tunnels pierced sheer rock to open up new districts, such as Copacabana. The Grand Exhibition of 1922 was intended to open wide the doors of international trade. It didn't happen, but the city benefited from the major tidy-up that preceded it. To this day it enjoys some lasting benefits from this non-event, among them the postcard-perfect pinnacle of hospitality, the Copacabana Palace Hotel.

Political ups and downs were punctuated by moments of tragedy, high comedy, and sheer insanity. It seemed that the young nation's adolescence was interminable. Maturity beckoned with the construction in 1960 of Brasília, the futuristic capital, planted smack in the middle of the country. The brainchild of charismatic President Juscelino Kubitschek, Brasília was intended to accelerate the country's political progress and give gravitas to government, but corruption, mismanagement, power-for-personal-gain and other symptoms of political immaturity continued to steal center stage. Finally, in 1964, the military called a halt and imposed their austere, nationalistic, and unpopular rule.

Left: Pedro II, a wise and scholarly ruler

The 1970s and 1980s were the ugly years of repression. Civil liberties were suspended, trade barriers isolated the country from international commerce, and censorship of the arts was a fact of life. Thinking people sought political, cultural and even physical asylum from the regime by leaving the country. Rio suffered: once the seat of power and style, it had lost its glamorous embassies to Brasília and its *joie de vivre* was dampened by the military.

Despite Brazil's darkest hours, during the military dictatorship, foundations were being laid for the road to democracy, and in 1989, for the first time, Brazilians were able to choose their president by direct vote. Fernando Collor de Mello's time in office started well enough, with an aggressive approach to inflation and innovative attempts to stabilize the currency, but ended in corruption, scandal, and embarrassment. Impeachment followed. But while Brasília boiled, Rio glowed, as it hosted the United Nations Conference on the Environment and Development, Eco-92. This went off without a hitch, and proved what we all know to be true: Rio can throw a wonderful party. The success of Eco-92 was providential, as Rio's image was already being affected by the rising crime rate, the chaos in the city, and a generally held – and often justifiable – view that it was not a place to go on vacation.

Creativity and the Cult of the Body

Even the adverse political climate was unable to halt the cultural, sporting, and artistic achievements of the Brazilian people. In the field of sport, what could be more eloquent than Brazil's unique situation as the only nation to win the World Cup soccer championship five times? In the arts, Paulo Coelho is among the world's best-selling authors, his work translated into 56 languages and available in 150 countries. On the musical front, the samba and the bossa nova are two styles of music that have become universally popular. The visual arts are a rich territory of local achievement, as can be seen at Rio's numerous cultural centers and the steady rise in prices achieved for the work of Brazilian artists at the world's auction houses. Brazilian movie-making has always been trend-setting, and the success of Walter

Above: view of Rio from the hills of Santa Teresa (1883), by Jorge Grimm

Salles's 1998 film *Central do Brasil* and the warts-and-all depiction of life in a Rio slum, *City of God* (2002), directed by Fernando Meirelles and Katia Lund, has been resounding.

Cariocas, as Rio residents are known, regard their bodies as works of art. They take them very seriously, which, when you consider how much these bodies are on display, is hardly surprising. The morning walk on the beach is a form of mind and body therapy sacred to many, and near-naked sun worship should perhaps rate as a national religion. There are busy gyms and fitness academies at every street corner. Brazil is at the cutting edge of cosmetic surgery, too, another indication of the lengths women and, increasingly, men, are prepared to go to in order to look their best.

Rio Today

Sadly, Rio suffers the scourge of many large cities, with a crime rate that can reach unacceptable levels. Overcrowding is partly to blame; despite the immensity of Brazil, over 80 percent of the population lives in cities. Homicide figures are shockingly high, and Brazil is second in the world's league table of deaths by violent means, with 27 out of 100,000 dying violently, as against 6.6 in the United States.

But the figures are not all bad. The birth rate is falling: the average number of children per woman was 6.3 in 1960, but 40 years later had dropped to a more manageable 2.3. Consequently, infant mortality rates have fallen dramatically, as have illiteracy rates. On the down side, this demographic shift means that a higher percentage of the population is elderly, which increases the demands on the already inadequate social services.

The 21st century dawned on a city that has reached a cultural maturity in keeping with its position as a major tourist destination. The revenue provided by tourism is important to Rio, and the state and municipal tourist boards are well-managed and efficient. A recent survey showed that over 90 percent of visitors to Brazil said they would like to return, and over 35 percent of them had centered their visit on Rio. No one is pretending that Rio does not have problems; traffic is chaotic and drug-related gang warfare commonplace. The divide between the haves and the have-nots has led to a huge security problem. But the majority of *cariocas* are fun-loving and hospitable. They value your visit, and most will go out of their way to help you.

HISTORY HIGHLIGHTS

1494 Spain and Portugal sign the territorial Treaty of Tordesillas.

1500 Pedro Álvares Cabral sails into Guanabara Bay, which he calls the River of January.

1532 Sugar cane is planted for the first time.

1533 Beginning of the slave trade; 4.5 million slaves enter Brazil over the next 350 years.

1565 The city of São Sebastião (later Rio de Janeiro) is founded by Estácio de Sá.

1567 The French are ousted and Rio becomes truly Portuguese.

1693 Gold is found in landlocked Minas Gerais, and shipped to Portugal from the ports of Paraty and Rio.

1721 The first coffee bushes are planted.

1760 Portuguese tradesmen discover Búzios.

1808 The Portuguese royal family takes up residence in Rio de Janeiro.

1821 Dom João VI returns to Portugal leaving his son, Pedro, as regent.

1822 Independence from Portugal is declared by Dom Pedro I.

1831 Pedro I abdicates in favour of his 5-year-old son who rules through a regency.

1832 Charles Darwin visits Rio de Janeiro aboard *The Beagle*.

1840 Dom Pedro II becomes emperor.

1850 The slave trade is outlawed.

1854 Brazil's first railway is inaugurated in Rio de Janeiro.

1884 Dom Pedro II goes up Corcovado mountain by rail.

1888 The Lei Aurea frees the last 723,719 slaves in Brazil.

1889 Proclamation of the republic.

1912 Sugar Loaf and Urca mountains are linked by cable-car.

1922 Grand Exhibition held in Rio.

1930 A coup brings to power Getúlio Vargas, populist and defender of the urban working class.

1933 *Flying down to Rio* premieres, with Fred Astaire and Ginger Rogers in supporting roles.

1940 A minimum wage is guaranteed to all workers.

1950 First broadcast goes out to 100 TV sets in the country. The inaugural soccer match is played at the Maracanã Stadium.

1960 The new city of Brasília is inaugurated as the nation's capital in place of Rio.

1962 The *bossa nova* is performed in Carnegie Hall, New York.

1964 Military coup. General Humberto de Alencar Castelo Branco becomes president. Brigitte Bardot discovers Búzios.

1974 Oil discovered off Rio's coast.

1989 Fernando Collor de Mello wins first presidential election by direct vote since 1961.

1992 United Nations Conference on the Environment and Development (Eco-92) held in Rio.

1994 The new currency, the *real* is created. Political scientist Fernando Henrique Cardoso is elected president. His *Plano Real* helps stabilize the currency.

1998 President Cardoso wins a second four-year term.

2001 Brazilian Gustavo Kuerten is ranked as the world's number one tennis player.

2002 Brazil wins its fifth World Cup soccer title.

2002 A former lathe operator and trade union leader Luis Inácio Lula da Silva (always known a Lula) is elected Brazil's president.

2007 Pan American Games to be held in Rio de Janeiro.

Left: a scene from the 2002 film *City of God*, set in the slums of Rio de Janeiro

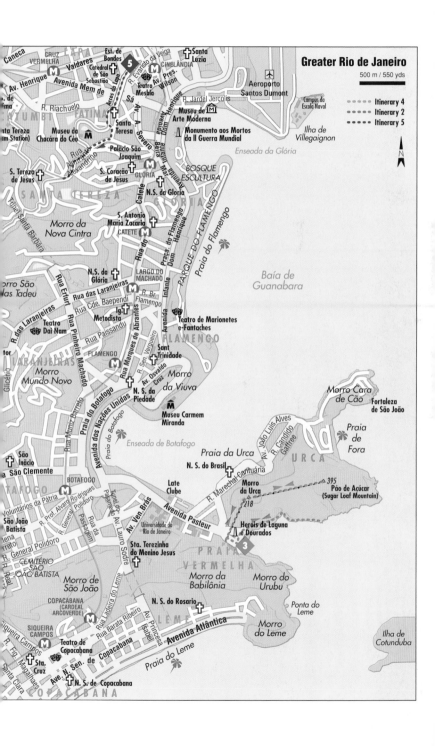

Greater Rio de Janeiro

500 m / 550 yds

⋯⋯⋯ Itinerary 4
⋯⋯⋯ Itinerary 2
⋯⋯⋯ Itinerary 5

Caneca
CRUZ VERMELHA
Valdares
Av. Henrique
Avenida Mem de
Est. de Bondes
Catedral de São Sebastião
R. Evaristo da Veiga
Santa Luzia
CINELÂNDIA
Teatro Mesbla
Pres. Wilson
Aeroporto Santos Dumont
R. de
ima
R. Riachuelo
Sá
R. Jardel Jercolis
Campus da Escola Naval
ATUMBI
FÁTIMA
Arcos da Lapa
R. A. Severo
Museu de Arte Moderna
nta Tereza (am Station)
Museu da Chácara do Céu
Santa Teresa
Monumento aos Mortos da II Guerra Mundial
Ilha de Villegaignon
Rua Almirante Alexandrino
Palácio São Joaquim
Enseada da Glória
S. Tereza de Jesus
S. Coração de Jesus
GLÓRIA
N.S. da Gloria
BOSQUE ESCULTURA
SANTA TEREZA
Morro da Nova Cintra
Catete
S. Antonio Maria Zacaria
CATETE
Baía de Guanabara
orro São las Tadeu
Rua Erfurt
N.S. da Glória
Rua das Laranjeiras
LARGO DO MACHADO
Infante
PARQUE DO FLAMENGO
Praia do Flamengo
R. das Laranjeiras
Rua Cde. Baependi
Metodista
R. Br. Flamengo
Teatro Dai Nam
Rua Pinheiro Machado
Rua Paissandu
Rua Marques de Abrantes
Avenida
Teatro de Marionetes e Fantaches
tor
LARANJEIRAS
FLAMENGO
Sant Trinidade
FLAMENGO
Morro Mundo Novo
R. Sen. Vergueiro
N. S. da Piedade
Av. Osvaldo Cruz
Morro da Viuva
Morro Cara de Cão
Fortaleza de São João
Praia da Urca
N. S. do Brasil
Av. João Luís Alves
R. Cândido Gaffree
Praia de Fora
Praia do Botafogo
Museu Carmem Miranda
URCA
São Inácio
a São Clemente
Avenida das Nações Unidas
Enseada de Botafogo
R. Marechal Cantuária
Morro da Urca
395
Pão de Açúcar (Sugar Loaf Mountain)
BOTAFOGO
Iate Clube
R. Mimi Barreto
Túnel do Pasmado
R. Prof. Alvaro Rodrigues
R. General Polidoro
218
TAFOGO
Voluntários da Pátria
Rua da Passagem
Av. Ven. Brás
Avenida Pasteur
Heróis de Laguna e Dourados
São João Batista
Universidade do Rio de Janeiro
ena rreto
R. General Polidoro
CEMITÉRIO SÃO JOÃO BATISTA
Rua Lauro Sodré
Sta. Terezinha do Menino Jesus
PRAIA
Santa Clara
Siqueira Campos
R. Fig. Magalhães
Morro de São João
COPACABANA (CARDEAL ARCOVERDE)
Rua Ladeira do Leme
N. S. do Rosario
VERMELHA
Morro da Babilônia
Morro do Urubu
Morro do Leme
Ponta do Leme
Ilha de Cotunduba
SIQUEIRA CAMPOS
Teatro de Copacabana
Rua Barata Ribeiro
Av. Princesa Isabel
LEME
Av. N. Sen. de Copacabana
Sta. Cruz
Avenida Atlântica
Avenida do Leme
Praia do Leme
Ave. N. Sen. de
N. S. de Copacabana
COPACABANA

City Itineraries

1. CENTRAL RIO *(see map, page 22)*

This midday walking tour takes in some of the city's busiest spots, and visits historic locations that still figure prominently in the everyday life of Rio, such as the Imperial Palace and St Benedict's Church and Monastery. There are plenty of pit stops for refreshment along the way. Appropriate relaxing points include the Atrium restaurant in the Paço Imperial and the food outlets in the Centro Cultural Branco do Brasil

This walk should not be undertaken on a Monday, when many of the recommended attractions are closed.

Why not get to know the historic city center of Rio de Janeiro the way the first real tourists did in the early 19th century? Just like João VI and the rest of the Portuguese royal family and court in 1808, your starting point could be the **Paço Imperial** (Imperial Palace; Tues–Sun noon–6pm; free) at Praça Quinze 48 on the corner of Rua Primeiro de Março, and easily reached by cab. A simple, symmetrical edifice, this building served as the first official residence of the Portuguese royal family – but not for very long, as they found the air too fetid and the surrounding streets too dirty for a longer stay.

In its time the palace has served many purposes, among them that of central post office, but it is now dedicated to the arts. It is a multi-purpose cultural center, with an always-interesting selection of exhibitions and performances. The restaurant offers excellent snack options, and the shops stock out-of-the-ordinary designer items.

When you re-emerge into the square, take a few minutes to visit the waterfront, overlooking the Bay of Guanabara. This is the point of departure for the frequent ferries to Niterói and Paquetá. Two equestrian statues dominate the square; one commemorates the victories of local hero General Osório (who defended the empire in the wars with Paraguay, 1864–70); the other has frozen the hapless Dom João VI in time, and in a place where he was never very happy. The Chafariz do Mestre Valentim is the city's old water source, and the area immediately around it has been excavated to reveal traces of colonial Rio's shore line.

Old Rio

Onward to the past. With your back to the bay, cross to the right of the square and enter the magical old world enclosed by the Arco do Teles, an archway that goes back to 1790. Banish the modern world and appreciate the narrow, cobbled streets and the charm of the rickety wrought-iron work. This is the **Travessa do Comércio**, as authentic a slice of old Rio as one could hope for. Behind

Left: the Paço Imperial with a modern backdrop
Right: fountain outside the Igreja de Candelária

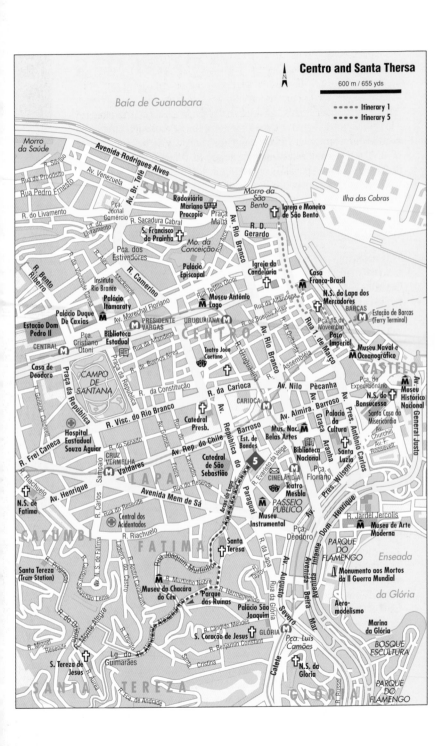

Centro and Santa Thersa

600 m / 655 yds

- - - - - Itinerary 1
- - - - - Itinerary 5

the old-fashioned façades, modern premises function as offices of various kinds. The almost-hidden entrance to No. 17, Casa Granado, home of the former apothecary to the royal family, conceals still-functioning, ultra-modern, open-plan offices. In the late afternoon, tables and chairs take over the entire street, and office workers kill a bit of time and a few beers while waiting for the worst of the rush hour to work itself out.

The street which crosses Travessa do Comércio is Rua do Ouvidor, and you need to turn left onto it to reach the **Igreja de Nossa Senhora da Lapa dos Mercadores** (Church of Our Lady of the Merchants; Mon–Sat 8am–2pm; free). This may well be the smallest church you will ever visit, accommodating a mere dozen people at a time. It was built by grateful merchants in 1747, and is considered a gem of baroque architecture.

Continuing on Rua do Ouvidor, make your way back to Rua Primeiro de Março, then turn right onto Rua Visconde de Itaboraí. At No. 20, at the end of the short block, you will see the **Centro Cultural Correios** (Post Office Cultural Center; Tues–Sun noon–7pm; free), on the corner. This unassuming building packs a punch in terms of content. It houses up to five temporary exhibitions at a time, always of the highest standard, beautifully showcased by perennially creative local designers. No boring rows of badly lit oil paintings here. Hardwood floorboards are polished to a mirror-like shine, occasionally lit by shafts of sunlight from the out-

side world. Rare and precious glimpses of the rooftops of old Rio can be spied from the windows; and the elevator is like a giant step back in time. There is a bar, a pocket theater, and an open patio where 'happenings' take place. And, of course, there's a post office.

Casa França-Brasil

Leaving the Centro Cultural Correios behind you, to your right, continue on down the cobbled street until you reach the **Casa França-Brasil** (Tues–Sun noon–8pm; free), which is also on your right. It was originally designed as a trading center for local produce, but it only served this humble purpose for a mere two years and by 1821 was already being used as a meeting place for politicians, just like the Roman forum it evokes. Nowadays, it houses exhibitions of many different kinds. Inside, you will experience a surprising architectural mix of neo-classical and Renaissance styles. The ceiling is impressive, and the flagstone floor ankle-breakingly irregular, so mind your step while you are gazing upwards.

Your next stop, across the tiny street in front of the Casa França-Brasil, is the seriously impressive and well air-conditioned **Centro Cultural Banco**

Right: a view of the tiny Nossa Senhora da Lapa dos Mercadores

do Brasil (Tues–Sun 10am–9pm; free), Rio's pride and joy. The former headquarters of the national bank was turned into a multi-purpose cultural center in 1989 and its success spawned several similar institutions around the city. The sheer grandiosity of the building, the wonderful natural light provided by the skylight roof, and the gracefully circular mezzanines make it a perfect backdrop for a wide variety of activities. These marbled halls host a theater, video screening rooms, a cinema, a bookshop, a concert hall, snack bars and tearooms as well as the most impressive exhibition sites in the city. Treat yourself, and take the elevator—a gilded cage if ever there was one—to any of the floors.

An average of 6,000 people visit the place daily, and peak attendance reaches 19,000 a day when a particularly popular exhibition is being staged. The Centro Cultural is certainly worth a visit; even if you do not particularly empathize with what you see or hear, you can admire the grandeur of its architecture and the creativity of all those involved in its inception and administration.

A Benedictine Treasure

As you leave the Centro Cultural Banco do Brasil, you are faced with the awesomely wide and frantically busy Avenida Presidente Vargas. To your left is the Igreja da Candelária. You can skip this, as a far more attractive church is just a walk away. Carry on down Rua Primeiro de Março, sticking to the sidewalk on the right-hand side. Cross over Rua Teófilo Otoni and Rua Visconde de Inhaúma, and you are in navy territory. Observe the number of uniform outfitters and flag makers across the road. Aim for a monstrous rubber tree, with hairy hanging roots, right on the sidewalk. Rua Primeiro de Março ends here, and turns left to become Rua Dom Gerardo.

Carry on until you reach No. 40, a nondescript lobby resembling many others you have passed on your walk. This one is different. At the rear, to the left, is an elevator. You want to go to the fifth floor, to visit the **Igreja e Mosteiro de São Bento** (St Benedict's Church and Monastery; tel: 2291-7122; daily 7–11am, 2.30–5.30pm; free). The elevator delivers you to a beautiful setting, home to one of Rio's most beloved churches. As you approach the building, surrounded by trees and singing birds, the portion to the right of the magnificent church gates is the secluded workplace of the Benedictine monks who still live in cloisters here. Obviously, it is off-limits for visitors. The church is famous for its sung masses, in the rich Gregorian tradition, and you may like to time your visit so that you can hear one. Early morning masses are particularly uplifting. Mass times are Sunday 8am, 10am (sung) and 6pm; Mon–Fri 7.15am (sung), 5pm (side chapel), and Saturday 7.15am (sung).

Above Left: inside the Centro Cultural Banco do Brasil. **Above Right:** statue of St Benedict
Right: colorful façades in Rua Primeiro de Março

The deceptively simple façade leads into an ornate and grandiose interior, filled with points of interest. One is immediately struck by the intricacy of the woodcarving and the amount of gold leaf that has been applied to the interior of the church. Each side chapel seems to outdo its neighbor in embellishment. Proceeding down the right-hand side of the church, you come across the chapel devoted to the luckless St Lawrence, roasted over glowing coals in AD 248, carrying the grille upon which he met his fiery end. The high altar is dedicated to Our Lady of Monserrat. To her right she is guarded by St Benedict and to her left, by the saint's beloved sister, St Scholastica. It seems fitting that these holy siblings should stand forever in each other's company; while they lived, they were allowed to meet only once a year.

An Unusual View

For a most unusual view of Rio, leave the church and veer off to the right, beyond the facilities and still within the compound of the church. Enter an uninviting-looking tunnel, and stick to the narrow sidewalk on your right. Soon you emerge into daylight, and before you is the Bay of Guanabara. Somehow, the fast-moving traffic on the overpass seems less hostile from this viewpoint. Carry on down the path to your left, through the grounds of the prestigious São Bento boys' school, and soon you'll be back on Rua Dom Gerardo, where you will have no problem in flagging a passing cab.

The Igreja de São Bento is a peaceful way to end what has been an eclectic itinerary, but a good introduction to the city, blending history with contemporary artistic output, and deafening traffic with the tranquillity of a church on a hill. Time to head back to your hotel.

2. CORCOVADO, THE MUSEUM OF NAIVE ART AND APOTHECARY'S SQUARE *(see map, pages 18–19)*

This half-day tour takes you to Cristo Redentor, one of the world's greatest landmarks, traveling by train through the rainforest. Come down to earth at the end with a visit to an endearing little museum, housing a fine and irreverent collection of naïve art, then move on for a glimpse of Rio in the olden days.

If going by cab, make it clear that you want the 'Estação do Trem do Corcovado, Rua Cosme Velho,' otherwise the driver may take you all the way to the top of the mountain, which you do not want.

The official name of Rio's most stunning monument is **Cristo Redentor** (Christ the Redeemer), and the mountain upon which it is perched is called Corcovado, which translates as 'hunchback.' The picturesque red train leaves from the no-less picturesque **Estação do Trem do Corcovado** (tel: 2558-1329; daily 8.30am–6.30pm; admission charge approx. $12) on Rua Cosme Velho 513, and has been doing so since 1884, when Emperor Dom Pedro II first made the trip. If paying by credit card, call ahead to ensure that the one you intend to use is acceptable, as things change. Children up to the age of five travel free, and those between the ages of five and 12 pay half fare.

Trains depart every half-hour, and the trip takes some 20 minutes; 360 passengers an hour can be transported, and there is generally a fast-moving line at the ticket counter. They normally only sell as many tickets as there are seats, so you don't have to worry about missing the train, or not getting a seat. If, on an exceptionally busy day, your ticket is for the next-but-one train, pop along to the International Museum of Naïve Art *(see page 29)*, to fill the time. A rudimentary pictorial history of the monument site can be viewed at the station before departure. The souvenirs are, ironically, among the

Above: Corcovado viewpoint

least attractive Rio has to offer – with the exception of the soccer memorabilia, which is the worst of all. You can stay at the top of the mountain for as long as you like, and board any train to come back down. Services at the top are basic, but there's a decent café/restaurant and clean toilets.

Try for a seat on the platform side, on the right as you look up to the statue, as there is a good photo opportunity as you approach the top. That said, when the train is full there is such a scramble for cameras and window space that few people actually get to record the shot they want. The seats are sheer wood, and quite slippery. Be prepared to knock knees with the person opposite, as space is tight.

Rainforest Sights and Smells

The train passes tantalizingly close to some run-down but attractive buildings before entering the forest. The only stop en route is at the Paineiras station, where you sit for a few minutes, waiting for the down train to pass; you can't disembark here. Paineiras belongs to the Federal Government, and has been many things in its time, including a private residence and a hotel. It was leased to a university in 1984, on the understanding that a hotel school would operate here. This failed to happen, and the building is now embroiled in a legal battle that started in 1990 and shows no signs of being resolved. Paineiras had its moment of glory in the 1970s, when the victorious Brazilian national soccer squad was based there.

From here, it's upwards into the **Floresta da Tijuca** (Tijuca Rainforest), the largest urban forest in the world. Much of the original forest was cleared in the middle of the 19th century and given over to coffee plantations. These did not prosper but left wide-open, unprotected tracts of land, provoking soil erosion and destroying the habitats of numerous animals, as well as affecting the city's water supply. Things reached such a state that the emperor undertook a pioneering environmental project in the area, the replanting of the Tijuca Rainforest. This was started in 1881, under the supervision of a certain Major Archer, who, with the help of half a dozen slaves, planted some 100,000 trees over a 13-year period. The result is a lush, damp, fern-filled forest floor below, and a canopy of rich green above. The train travels at a mere 15kmh (9½mph) on the way up, so you can really get a feel for the variety of vegetation.

Mosses and ferns cling to the permanently damp rocks. The enormous, ugly fruit of the durian trees hang patiently from the barks of the trees until it is time to splatter to the ground in a ripe, foul-smelling heap. From every patch of soil, something sprouts. The brightly coloured faces of busy lizzies (*Impatiens*) are everywhere, and it may come as no surprise to know that they are called 'shameless Marys' in Portuguese.

Right: Corcovado station

The Cristo Redentor Monument

When you get to the top of the mountain, there is an unruly, excited rush to disembark. Let the crowds go ahead of you and take it easy – there is nothing to hurry for. Getting to the base of the statue was, in years gone by, quite an arduous experience, but things have been made much easier for visitors by the installation of elevators and escalators. While essential for the elderly or people with disabilities, the elevators are not otherwise much help, as they only carry 13 passengers at a time and standing around waiting for them can be quite tiring. You will do far better to climb the first steps at a gentle pace, and then board the escalators that take you up to the highest of highs. It is often windy up here and skirts will swirl, as will swarms of dead wasps that have flown too close to the spotlights.

The statue itself is impressive, but you are almost too close to appreciate the detail and magnitude of it. It has been here since 1931, when it was hauled up in pieces on the train. Made of reinforced concrete clad in soapstone, the monument was made in France under the supervision of Paul Landowski. Its dimensions are staggering: 30m (98ft) high, sitting on an 8-m (26-ft) pedestal. The distance between the statue's fingertips is 30m (98ft), and the entire monument weighs 1,145 tons.

At the base of the statue is a tiny chapel, dedicated to Nossa Senhora Aparecida, the patron of Brazil. It is seriously at odds with the grandiosity all around it and not what one would expect from this exceptional religious site. The altar is tackily decorated with artificial flowers and the floor littered with coins, thrown as offerings by the faithful.

Seeing is Believing

The views cannot be described, only experienced. From this height you can appreciate just what an enormous city Rio is, and how tightly it is squeezed between the mountains and the sea. You also realize that you, as a visitor, will not see it all, especially the industrial zones and the badlands towards and beyond the airport. You can see that the Rodrigo de Freitas lagoon is very large indeed, and that Ipanema occupies a crowded, narrow band of land. You can measure how much prime real estate the Jockey Club occupies, and how green the Jardim Botânico is. In the other direction, you can recognize how ambitious an undertaking the construction of the Rio–Níteroi Bridge was, and what a difference it has made to the city. The flying saucer shape of Maracanã soccer stadium sticks out a mile, as do the vast expanses of densely occupied land, often overhung by a pall of polluted air. Make your way slowly around, using the maps on the railings to get your bearings. These are especially useful if there is a sudden change in the weather and you are cloaked in mist, unable to see beyond the maps themselves. If this should happen, and it frequently does, just be patient, read a book and wait a while, as the clouds rush past and views should be revealed in no time at all.

Left: Cristo Redentor monument. **Above Right:** graffiti outside the museum. **Right:** view of Lagoa Rodrigo de Freitas

You join a line to board the train for the slightly slower return journey. You may find that a certain sense of anti-climax pervades – or is it the aftermath of exhilaration? After all, you have just seen one of the world's greatest sights.

Irreverent Art

As you come out of the train station, turn left for MIAN – the **Museu Internacional de Arte Naïf** (International Museum of Naïve Art; Tues–Fri 10am–6pm, Sat–Sun and holidays noon–6pm; minimal admission charge), a museum overflowing with vibrant color and fun. Note that the entrance charge is halved if you have been on, or are about to go on, the Corcovado train.

The term naïve is applied, generally speaking, to art as practiced by the self-taught, free from the influences of formal artistic trends or schools. Brazil takes its place with France, the former Yugoslavia, Haiti and Italy among the world's top five exponents of the style. Here, in this intimate little museum, you will see the best Brazil has to offer. As you walk in, you are immediately hit by the impact of a vast canvas, measuring 4m by 7m (13ft by 23ft), by Lia Mittarakis, entitled *Rio de Janeiro, I Like You, I Like Your Happy People,* a quotation from one of the city's favorite old-time waltzes. Wander around to capture the lack of inhibition, the undisciplined use of color and the sheer cheek of the works on display. Another quotation catches the eye, this one by Einstein: 'Imagination is more important than knowledge,' a judgement that perfectly sums up the concept of naïve art.

One unmissable work is Aparecida Azedo's *Five Centuries of Brazil.* Viewed from a mezzanine level, it measures a staggering 1.40m by 24m (4.5ft by 78.5ft). Key events in Brazilian development are shown with bold simplicity, and explanations of the historical scenes depicted are given on the railings of the mezzanine.

Downstairs is a collection of international art, and although much of it originates in South America it seems to lack the vigor of the Brazilian works. In fact, some of it seems rather depressing and only serves to emphasize the joy that emanates from the local works.

Before leaving the museum, make the most of the glassed-in shop, which has high-quality, artistic items on sale. Excellent reproductions of Brazilian art, as well as some originals, make easy-to-pack mementos of your day.

If a trip up Corcovado gave you a feel for the geography of Rio de Janeiro, then a trip to the MIAN will have provided a perfect glimpse into the history, culture, and pervading mood of the city.

Apothecary's Square

As you leave the MIAN, turn left again and a little way up the hill, at Rua Cosme Velho 815, you come to the **Largo do Boticário** (Apothecary's Square). This appealing little piece of old Rio was put together in the 1920s in neo-colonial style with materials taken from demolition sites in the center of the city. What it lacks in authenticity it more than makes up for in charm. The houses are privately owned, and therefore cannot be visited, but the square is a perfect stop for a photo opportunity and a few moments of quiet contemplation.

3. SUGAR LOAF MOUNTAIN AND PISTA CLAUDIO COUTINHO WALK *(see pullout map)*

This half-day itinerary starts with a refreshing walk in picture-postcard scenery along the Pista Claudio Coutinho, and then takes you on a cable-car ride up to the Pão de Açúcar – Sugar Loaf Mountain.

If you are paying by credit card, remember to call the Sugar Loaf office ahead of time (tel: 2546-8400) to check card acceptability.

Your point of departure is **Praia Vermelha** (Red Beach), so-named for the dark, reddish color of its sand. The first thing that will strike you is the number of people here in military uniform. That's because you are in the armed forces' Rio de Janeiro headquarters; if you don't feel safe here, you won't feel safe anywhere. To the left of the beach, as you face it, you will see the Gabriela Mistral infant school – Mistral (1889–1957) was a revered Chilean poet and teacher who was awarded the Nobel Prize for Literature in 1945. To the left of the school is the entrance to the **Pista Claudio Coutinho** (daily 6am–6pm; free), a walk named in honor of the Brazilian

Left: Praia Vermelha with Sugar Loaf in the background

3. sugar loaf mountain   *31*

soccer team's trainer, who died in a diving accident in the area. This is one of Rio's lesser-known treasures, and is administered by the army. It is preserved from the intrusions of modern life by the prohibition of bicycles, cars, motorcycles and skates; the natural wildlife is kept safe by the no-pets policy. The walk is only 1.25km (¾ mile) long, but if you are a nature lover you will wish that it went on forever.

Natural Wonders

A paved pathway hugs the mountainside. To your right, the sea beats against the barnacle-covered rocks; to your left, the abundant fertility of the rainforest is punctuated by the bareness of granite – bare but not barren, as bromeliads bloom comfortably on the sheer rocks. Early on in the walk, you will come across a grotto, to your left, dedicated to Our Lady of the Conception, patron saint of the Brazilian military. Notice how the ferns sprout enthusiastically from the rocky altar. If you look back to your right you get a great view of Praia Vermelha.

Hummingbirds dart in and out of the light in dive-bombing movements that are hard to catch on film but wonderful to see. Gentle, hissing squeaks from the trees indicate the presence of another form of life: marmosets, always playfully curious, popping their white-tufted ears out of their tree homes to check out the passing human traffic. Weigh-

ing a mere 240g (8.5oz), these little creatures hate the cold so they are in their element here, and, provided they can avoid joining the food chain via the ever-watchful birds of prey, they can live for up to 20 years.

At all times of the year, the vegetation on the walk is breathtaking: black-eyed susans, pierced monsteras, giant elephant-ear philodendrons, blue gingers and masses of pinky-purple epidendrum orchids all thrive in this perfect environment. Brazilwood trees have been planted on the sea side of the walk; these slow-growing giants will one day create an impressive avenue. Fruit trees do well here, too, including mango, papaya and avocado. The birds know this and are present in great number and variety. The yellow waist-coats of the great kiskadees are everywhere and even if you cannot see them, you can hear their rackety calls. Pairs of powder-blue sayaca tanagers dance gracefully through the trees. The real prize, though, is the blood-red Brazilian tanager, one of the most beautiful birds in the world. If you are lucky enough to see one, you will never forget it.

The walk ends rather abruptly at an ugly concrete beacon, beyond which is a dangerous trail leading up the rocks. In fact, all along the walk are the starting points of hikes of varying degrees of difficulty. Do not undertake any of these hikes without the assistance of a proper guide *(see page 90 for details of companies that specialize in adventurous activities)*. All that remains now is to retrace your steps, enjoying the walk all over again as you do so.

When you arrive at Praia Vermelha, head for the building at the opposite

Right: a marmoset in Pista Claudio Coutinho

end of the beach. Although this is a military club, it is open to the public, and is a delightful place to have a snack and drink and put your feet up. Beyond the enclosed, noisy dining room is a shaded open-air area. It is open from 11am–1am, and there is live music at night.

Sugar Loaf

With your back to the sea, proceed to the far left of the impressive square, and aim for the main attraction, Rio's great emblem, the **Pão de Açúcar** (Sugar Loaf; daily 8am–10pm; admission charge), which was supposedly named for its resemblance in shape to the cones of pressed sugar exported to Europe in colonial days. Coincidentally, the early inhabitants of the Rio area, the Tamoio Indians, called the mountain Pau-nh-açuquä, which means 'high, pointed mountain standing alone.' It doesn't take a linguist to perceive the similarities between the Portuguese and Tamoio names for the famous rock.

The Sugar Loaf cable-car system has been in operation since 1912. At the time of its construction, only two other cable-cars were in existence: Mount Ulia in Spain, crossing 280m (920ft), and the Wetterhorn cable-car in the Swiss Alps, crossing 560m (1,840ft). Cars leave from Praia Vermelho station, where tickets are sold, every half hour, or whenever the full complement of 75 passengers is reached, and they run from 8am to 10pm. The ticket price is approximately US$10; children under the age of five travel free, and those between five and 12 pay half fare. The journey is a two-stage one, the first stop is the Morro da Urca (Urca Hill), followed by Sugar Loaf Hill itself. Hang on to your ticket, as you need to show it at every stage. Each part of the journey takes approximately three minutes, traveling at an average speed of 8m (26ft) per second.

The waiting area beyond the ticket barrier at ground level has very limited seating and no shops, so if you envisage a longish wait, stay the other side

of the barrier. Visitors in wheelchairs or with impaired mobility will find this tour practically impossible, but there are plans to make the whole site disabled-friendly in the near future.

From the first stop, **Morro da Urca**, you begin to see the city take shape below you. If you are a high flyer, this is the place to book your helicopter flight. Helisight has been circling these skies since 1970, and provides a safe and exciting service. Reservations can be made ahead of time by phone (tel: 2511-2141 or 2542-7895). If the Morro da Urca strikes you as being a great place for a party, you are quite right, as all kinds of events are held here. Inquire what the evening fixtures are, so that you can plan ahead for an unforgettable experience.

Reaching the Summit

Onward to Sugar Loaf mountain itself, over the thick canopy of trees. Relax when you reach the top and take it easy; time seems to stand still at this altitude. Indulge in the luxury of taking it easy, maybe reading a book or writing postcards, with one of the world's most exhilarating views before you. From this height the city is uncannily silent and almost still; it is like looking at a photograph.

Striding authoritatively across the bay is the stunning bridge linking Rio to Niterói. Britain's Queen Elizabeth II attended the ceremony marking the start of construction work on it in 1968, and the bridge was officially opened

to traffic six years later. The statistics are impressive. The bridge is 13.25km (8½ miles) in length, of which almost 9km (5½ miles) are over the water, and it soars to 72m (236ft) at its highest point. Pre-construction studies suggested that traffic would flow at the rate of 15,500 vehicles a day. Nowadays, some 115,000 commuters use the bridge every day.

If your shopping instincts remain intact even in this rarefied atmosphere, you will be pleased with the quality of souvenirs to be had at the top of Sugar Loaf Mountain. They are an improvement on the tacky offerings for sale at the mountain's lofty rival, Corcovado.

Despite being at the pinnacle of a very pointed mountain, there is walking to be done. Aim for the facilities (yes, there are some, you may be pleased to learn) and go down the steps. A very steep path – you should hang on to the guide ropes on either side – takes you into the (relative) wilderness, which is complete with more marmosets, and dark groves of bamboo. You can settle down at one of the many picnic tables to take a rest and breathe in the stunning views and the majestic setting. When you eventually retrace your steps and make landfall back at sea level, Rio's layout and its chaotic beauty will make much more sense to you.

Above Left: cable-car up the mountain. **Left:** the great sweep of Botafogo Bay
Above Right: Morro da Urca belvedere

4. BOTANICAL GARDENS *(see map, page 36)*

A three-hour visit to the Jardim Botânico, one of the world's most important botanical gardens and research centers.

For this itinerary, take a cab to the vehicle entrance, not the twin-tower pedestrian entrance in the middle of the palm avenue. You need good walking shoes, insect repellent, sunscreen and a hat.

The **Jardim Botânico** (Botanical Gardens; tel: 2294-9349; daily 8am–5pm; minimal admission charge) is at Rua Jardim Botânico 1008. Over 6,000 plant species thrive on its 189 hectares (467 acres), which are also home to more than 120 species of birds. At certain times of the year, multi-lingual guides are on hand to show you around, and if you have a real interest in the plant world you will definitely benefit from their expert knowledge.

A Royal Creation

The garden was born of a king's desire for a decent cup of tea, improbable though that may sound. Established in 1808 by Dom João VI – as were so many things in the city – the garden was intended as a nursery where exotic

imports such as tea and spices could be tested and eventually acclimatized to the local conditions. In contrast to current bans on the importation of plants, in those days the practice was encouraged and tax incentives were made available to those who wanted to bring new plants into the country. Since the early 19th century, the garden has grown to become one of the most important centers for botanical research in the world, as well as the city's favorite recreation area, visited by thousands of people each year.

You will encounter brilliantly colored heliconia plants and crazy cannon ball trees, also known as monkey's apricots. Busy lizzies *(Impatiens)* are everywhere. Look at the tops of the trees for some surprises: bromeliads in the canopy provide perfect bathtubs for birds. You have to be quick to snap the darting hummingbirds with your camera, and lucky to capture the toucans. Human biodiversity is also present: joggers, meditators, lovers and bridal parties, as this is a favourite spot for wedding photos.

Starting the Walk

Start at the pretty Café Botânica, which is overhung with the elaborate, slipper-shaped flowers of the clock vine, and with a Brazil-nut tree just in front. This is a good place to buy bottled water, and to get a snack when you return. Clean and welcoming toilet facilities are located here, as well. You set off to your right on to Aléia (Avenue) João Gomes, and then take a left on to Aléia Warming. This is not a reference to global warming, but an homage to a Danish botanist of that name who was active in Brazil in the 1860s. The massive mango trees close in on you, blocking out the sunlight.

Above: the Botanical Garden is a popular place for wedding photos
Above Right: the central fountain. **Right:** a thatched Amazon-style hut

Cross over Aléia Custódio Serrão, and soon you will reach a small hillock topped by a stone summer house. Here the royal family enjoyed their picnics at a giant stone table. You can check the time on the sundial. Bright splashes of color are added by the mussaendas, ixoras and plumbago. The lake lies before you, with the giant lily pads of the *Vitória regias,* resembling saucers, floating on the surface, but firmly rooted at the bottom of the lake. Birds cavort above you, plucking insects out of the air. Note the yellow-breasted, noisy, great kiskadees, who occasionally dive for fish, too.

Carnivorous Plants

Continue down Aléia Pizzaro, leaving the lake behind you to your left, and get to know the carnivorous plants housed just ahead of you. Venus fly traps, pitcher plants and sticky plants; they are rarely pretty, but always fascinating. Turn right onto Aléia Freire Alemão, shaded by dense bamboo. Russian composer Nikolai Rimsky-Korsakov was especially impressed by these bamboos when he saw them on his round-the-world naval cruise in 1862. Look out for the darting movements of the spotted rail – called a water chicken (*frango d'água*) in Portuguese – whose haunt this is.

The next right turn takes you along the Aléia Barbosa Rodrigues, lined with the imperial palms which are the hallmark of the garden. Straight ahead is the impressive central fountain, made in England, paying homage to music, art, science and poetry. To the left of the fountain is a majestic *sumauma* tree, with jutting buttress roots. Antonio Carlos Jobim, the revered local hero responsible for composing *The Girl from Ipanema* in the 1960s and for putting the bossa nova on the world scene, loved this spot, a fact which is remembered with a plaque.

city itineraries

Japanese Gardens

Straight ahead of you, the traffic whizzing past on Rua Jardim Botânico can be seen and heard. Avoid this intrusion by taking a left turn, which leads to a small roundabout crowned by a chunky palm. Turn right, and cross Aléia Karl Glass. Suddenly and unexpectedly the fertile opulence of the tropics is replaced by the precision and calm of the Orient. The Japanese Garden is an exotic microcosm, complete with wisteria, box hedges, a lotus pond and stunning, sculpted granite blocks whose plinths are mondo grass, native to Japan and Korea.

Crossing over the bridge and Aléia Barão de Capanema, you are back in Brazil with a jolt, smack in the middle of the rainforest. A typical, thatched Amazon dwelling perches on the lakeside, where a sculpted fisherman in a floppy hat sits for ever, patiently waiting for a fish to take his bait. Rampant greenery borders the lake.

Medicinal Trees

Leaving the Amazon behind you, take the Aléia Campos Porto, along which you will see a stunning avenue of giant Amazonian trees. These trees are *pau mulattos* or *mulateiros*, and what makes them special is their ability to completely shed their bark every year. When new, the bark is like polished bronze, ending up dun colored when it is ready to be shed. The Amazonian Indians have multiple uses for this readily available material: topically, it is used to treat wounds, while a concentrated tisane taken regularly is used to cure diabetes. Other tribes anoint themselves with a decoction of the

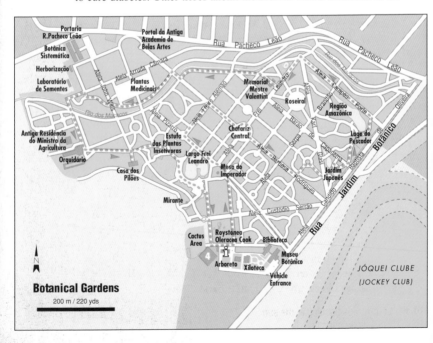

Botanical Gardens
200 m / 220 yds

city itineraries

bark: as it dries on their skin it forms a barrier against parasites and fungal infections. *Mulateiros*, then, are not only beautiful trees; in the right hands, they are extremely useful.

When you reach the end of the Aléía Campos Porto, there is an attractive fountain. Turn left onto Aléía Frei Leandro, aiming for the summer house, and admiring the line of spindly clove trees along the way. In summer, tiny pink cloves cover the ground, ready for collecting and drying. The cool, peaceful summer house, with angels' trumpets on gate duty, is a memorial to Valentim da Fonseca e Silva (1745–1813), usually known as Mestre Valentim, the sculptor responsible for most of the statuary in the garden. Turn right onto Aléía Barão de Capanema; when it turns left into Aléía Brade, there are some toilet facilities. Follow the Rio dos Macacos (Monkey River), where you will see haughty but dumb egrets wading, any number of rufous-bellied thrushes, and you may well encounter toucans.

The Research Institute

Take a left when you hit Aléía Barbosa Rodrigues and cross over the river; turn left again, and follow the river. To your right are the ruins of a gunpowder factory (also established by João VI), which blew up in 1831; only the bare walls and the gate remain. Within, there are swings for the children, restrooms and a café. Rejoin the path, crossing over Aléía John Wills. To your right are the offices of the Research Institute – the organization that makes Rio's Jardim Botânico more than just a garden and arboretum. From the pergola over the path hangs one of the most bizarre plants you are likely to encounter. It's the *Aristolochia elegans*, called the Dutchman's Pipe, though any number of more descriptive names come to mind when this monster is in flower.

Cross over a steep, planked bridge, noting the epiphytes (plants that derive their nutrients from the air) clinging to the electricity wires above. Here you can visit the bromeliad house, where you will see what a multiplicity of interesting relatives the domestic pineapple has. To your right is an attractive collection of Amazon vegetation, of which the ferns are the highlights.

Orchids and Brazilwood Trees

Out into the daylight again, turn right, passing the mustard-colored administration building on your right. Observe the old man's beard, or Spanish moss, cloaking the trees. Surprisingly, this strange plant is yet another member of the pineapple family. Next is the orchid house, with the exotic specimens clearly labelled. At the rear of the orchid house is a peaceful lawned area where you'll find a little bit of paradise. Take a seat on the bench and contemplate a wonderful view of Corcovado.

You need to retrace your steps back through the orchids to reach Aléía Alberto Lofgren. Your next stop is the archeological display at the **Casa dos Pilões**, where huge millstones

Above Left: turtles basking in the sun
Right: a tree-lined avenue

guard the entrance, which is shaded by Malay apple *(jambeiro)* trees. In season, they drop needle-like, shocking-pink petals, which form a carpet. Back on the main path, you will soon be at the lake, bordered by banana trees and a species known as travelers' palms. To your right is a stone structure, veiled in hanging ferns. Take a right here and meet the giants of the Brazilian tree world, lining the right-hand side of the avenue: the ironwood tree, noble mahogany and the brazilwood tree that gave the country its name.

The café is once again in sight now, but take a few minutes more to visit the **Sensorial Garden** up the path to your right. Designed with the visually impaired in mind, the garden is planted with a clever mix of scented and textured plants that can be 'seen' by the eyes of the blind – their hands. The signs are in Braille. A visit here makes you all the more grateful for your own senses.

5. SANTA TERESA AND CHACARA DO CÉU
(see map, page 22)

A tour of one of Rio's most picturesque and bohemian neighborhoods, Santa Teresa, reached by a tram ride across the Arcos de Lapa.

Get a taxi to the tram station. Note that the Chácara do Céu, the highlight of this visit, only opens at noon and is closed on Tuesday.

Getting to Santa Teresa is half the fun, so make sure you go on the tram, or *bonde*, as it is called. You start from the **Estação do Bonde** in the humming center of downtown Rio. Be firm with the cab driver who takes you there about where you want to go, as he would no doubt prefer to take

you up the mountainous roads himself. The tram has acquired a reputation over the years for being dangerous, and it is a pickpocket's dream come true, so hang on to your belongings, which should be kept to a minimum. The station seems like a little bit of garden in the bustle of the business core of Rio, where the buildings tower above you. Tickets for the tram are ludicrously cheap, and the simple, old-fashioned vehicle seems to have been left over from days gone by. All aboard, and amid much shouting and carrying-on by the driver and conductor, off you trundle. Quaint it may be, but quiet it isn't. Hang on tight; it isn't hard to imagine bouncing right out of the tram. Velcro on your behind, or rodeo experience, would not go amiss here.

The tram clanks its way over the magnificent **Arcos da Lapa**, the disused aqueduct that strides over the Lapa region. Vertigo sufferers should try not to look down. Before long, you are clanking up toward Santa Teresa.

The views are magnificent, a different take on the familiar contours made famous through postcard images of the city. Notice how, in this land of natural plenty, vegetation springs from every patch, and even from the roof tiles themselves.

Above: the tram crosses the Arcos da Lapa

city itineraries

Ruins and Restoration

Tell the tram driver you are going to the museu (pronounced *moo-zeu*) and he will drop you off at the Curva do Curvelo. Make for the well-signposted **Parque das Ruínas** (Ruins Park), a 5-minute walk away. This is the former home of society hostess Laurinda Santos Lobo, whose parties, held on the fourth day of every month, attracted the likes of dancer Isadora Duncan and writer Anatole France, as well as the cream of Rio society. On her death in 1946, the building was abandoned, and fell into disrepair. By 1995 it was truly a wreck, and architects Ernani Freire and Sonia Lopes rose to the challenge of restoring it, without, as they put it, 'frightening the ghosts away.' They seem to have succeeded, for the place has an extraordinary feel to it, combining ancient with modern, crumbling bricks with tubular steel. Cross the giant sundial in the courtyard floor and stand on the stone benches for some wonderful views. As you leave, look back up at the railings that surround the property: back-lit photographs are displayed here, a novel way to stage a photographic exhibition.

Little Villa in Heaven

Your next stop is at Rua Murtinho No. 93, the **Chácara do Céu** (Little Villa in Heaven; tel: 2224-8981; Wed–Mon noon–5pm; minimal admission charge, free on Wed). It is right next door to the Parque das Ruínas, although you have to go round the corner to reach the entrance. This is the former residence of Raymundo Castro Maya (1894–1968), a stylish industrialist, entrepreneur and art collector, who also gave wonderful parties. Most of the house is laid out as a museum, and provides a personal view of life at the top in the middle of

Above: colorful façades in Santa Teresa
Right: view of the city from the top of the hill

the last century. It is fitting that the home of this man, who loved Rio and did so much for the city, should be open to visits by all. There are treasures all around, not least of which is the solid wooden staircase, made of *peroba* wood, now on the endangered-species list. The house was built in 1954 and was considered fiercely modern for its times. The effect of natural daylight can be experienced in every room and the integration of the house with its surrounding garden is complete.

Private Collection

Works by Picasso, Dali, Matisse and Miró are dotted around the walls. While the collection is no rival for major international museums, it is still thrilling to see works by artists such as these hanging on the walls of what is, in effect, a private home. The Dufy in the library is a gem; it shows a French beach, complete with tricolor flapping in the wind, and the beach-goers are all decked out in shirts and ties and long dresses – a far cry from Ipanema.

Castro Maya's two passions, Rio and art, have resulted in one of the most important collections of Brazilian art to be found anywhere. Works by Guinard, Iberê Camargo and the now very collectable Di Cavalcanti are all on display, and the Chácara also houses the largest collection of works by Cândido Portinari (1903–62), possibly Brazil's best-known artist. There is also a collection of watercolors and drawings by Jean Baptiste Debret (1768–1848), a French artist whose work brought to life the Brazil of the early 19th century. For the foreign visitor, the pictures of Rio hold special appeal, as you can see the familiar outlines of the mountains uncluttered by development. You can experience this in the stunning Thomas Ender oil painting (1848) at the top of the stairs. There is a sister museum, the Museu do Açude, in the Floresta da Tijuca (Estrada do Açude 764, Alto do Boa Vista).

The garden is a magical spot, with 360 degree views of Rio. The city is so close that you feel you can touch it, but far enough away that it is silent.

city itineraries

The garden is home to numerous birds, and also to some evil-looking but harmless lizards. The mango tree dominates the lawn, and the flamboyant tree splashes its flame-colored summer blossom against the austerely modern lines of the house.

The Tram Museum and Shopping Opportunities

Allow yourself time to return to the front door, at the bottom of the stairs, because the little shop has some tasteful souvenirs. Afterwards, make your way back to the tram at the Largo dos Guimarães, which is the downtown area of Santa Teresa. There are signs to the two-roomed **Museu do Bonde** (daily 9am–4.30pm; free), down a cobbled street, Rua Carlos Brant (No. 14). While not exactly overflowing with interest, it is worth a stop if you are interested in trams or railways – the memorabilia here harks back to the days when trolleys were pulled by mules – or want to see some excellent photos of Rio in the olden days. Take a good look at the gate to see what interesting effects can be created with bits of twisted wire and steel.

It is probably time for something to eat by now, unless you had a very early lunch before you started this itinerary, so make your way back to the main road. En route you will pass some attractive old-fashioned shops, general stores really, selling just about everything from buckets and brooms to candles and clothes pins, the sort of shops where they still polish the oranges before piling them high in neat pyramids.

Santa Teresa has always been an arty place, and this is reflected in the colorful handicraft shops, selling oversized wooden avocados and clay figurines of unfailingly smiling, fat little people. There are plenty of light and portable items for sale, so this might be the time to stock up on gifts or mementos to take back home with you.

Eating Options

Eating options are plentiful, inexpensive and right to hand, clustering around the Largo dos Guimarães. The popular **Adega do Pimenta** at Rua Almirante Alexandrino 296 has a decidedly German accent, serving all forms of *wurst* (sausage), as well as rabbit and duck dishes. Like the Chácara do Céu, whose visitors represent many of its customers, it is closed on Tuesday.

Close by, at No. 316B, is **Bar do Arnaudo** (closed Monday), where the food and atmosphere are both distinctly Brazilian. Sun-dried beef with pumpkin and *sarapatel*, a spicy stew made with turtle meat or pork, are on the menu, as are some more conventional dishes. The tastefully decorated **Sobrenatural**, on the same stretch of Almirante Alexandrino, at No. 432, offers a broader menu and prides itself on its excellent fish dishes.

To get back to sea level and the heart of Rio, you can either flag down a passing cab (there are usually plenty of them around), or test your nerves on the tram once more.

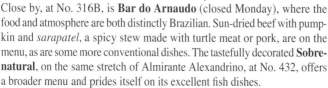

Above Left: Santa Teresa rooftops. **Left:** a shop selling everything you need
Right: a trip on the old yellow tram is a Rio experience

Excursions

1. CASA DO PONTAL AND BURLE MARX GARDENS
(see map, pages 44–45)

A trip along the beach at Barra da Tijuca to a rare exhibition of Brazilian popular art, and then on to the home of the landscape architect, Roberto Burle Marx. The itinerary is approximately a 70-km (45-mile) round trip from the mosque-like dome in downtown Barra da Tijuca.

The best idea is to hire a cab for the day; buses do not connect the suggested sites and the chances of getting lost if driving yourself are considerable. The cost of the cab should not be more than about US$40, though it will be more if you sensibly decide to linger over lunch in Guaratiba. The best days to do this trip are Tuesday to Friday – the two main sites are open on weekends, but the restaurants get crowded. The Sítio Burle Marx walk is accompanied by an official guide and must be reserved in advance (tel: 2410-1412); it is not entirely suitable for people with disabilities.

Your destination is the end of the beach, the **Praia da Barra**, and it makes sense to get there via the coast road, also called Praia da Barra. The views are stunning: endless lengths of white sand on your left and messy mangroves on your right. The Casa do Pontal is well-signposted, and to get to it you pass a world of contrasts, with private mansions sharing space with the humble dwellings of local workers. Some driveways are lined with security cameras and guards, others with mutts and chickens scratching in the earth.

Casa do Pontal

Jacques Van de Beuque was a French World War II hero who came to Brazil in the late 1940s. His passion for local crafts resulted in one of the biggest collections of Brazilian folk art in existence, amassed over a period of 50 years. It is housed in the **Museu Casa do Pontal** (Estrada do Pontal 3295, Recreio; tel: 2490-3278; Tues–Sun 9am–5pm; small admission charge), which Van de Beuque built in 1974. No one sums up what it's all about better than the man himself: 'The Casa do Pontal is dedicated to the country which took me in and allowed me to live my dream – a dream I hope to convey to our visitors. In a corrupt world, full of violence and hatred, it is a great comfort to be able to enter a universe created by the skilled hands of humble and honest artists.'

   Into this universe you go, visiting different areas of Brazil and peeking into local traditions and festivals. The entire population of this vast and diverse country seems to be present in the displays. The doctor, the lawyer, the policeman, country folk, *Carnaval* samba dancers, saints and

Left: Praia do Prainha. **Right:** balloon seller on the beach.
Following Pages (left and right): Sítio Burle Marx

sinners, are all represented here. The clay figures capture, with great humor in many cases, the simplicity of the lives of the artists who created them. Even death is represented, in a poignant, darkened corner of this professionally laid-out exhibition. Less gloomy is the collection of erotica, discreetly lodged behind a closed door. You leave the Casa do Pontal feeling that you have visited Brazil not through the artificial lens of the glossy brochure but through the eyes of the people who live, work and play in it.

Gardener *par excellence*

Now you wind your way back to Avenida das Américas, climb the hill at the end of it, and descend into the area of **Guaratiba**. Your destination is to the left, so your cab driver, who will know the way, should double back at a gas station, and take a right turn to the clearly marked **Sítio Burle Marx** (Estrada de Guaratiba 2019; tel: 2410-1412; Tues–Sun; pre-booked accompanied walks lasting approximately 1½ hours depart from the main building at 9.30am and 1.30pm; small admission charge). Rendezvous with your guide for a visit to the home of another man who was passionate about

Brazil – Roberto Burle Marx (1909–94). A multi-talented artist, he is credited with bringing about a revolution in landscape art that has influenced the treatment of outdoor space the world over.

Burle Marx set up home here in 1949 because he was tired of relying on commercial plant suppliers to provide specimens for his designs, and decided to grow his own. He was an avid collector and visited far-away places, often in the company of British botanical painter, Margaret Mee, to learn about plants and the micro-environments necessary to their survival. Burle Marx brought back many rare plant specimens from his travels – some have been named after him – but far from being a predator, he was keen to help them survive, and propagated them in his nursery.

The Sítio offers contrasting environments, including sun, shade, rocks, and running and still water, so an enormous variety of plants and groupings can be observed. Burle Marx's insight into texture, color, form and weight can be seen all around. The house is a treat apart. Here you will see other evidence of Burle Marx's creativity, through his paintings, textile art and

magnificent floral installations, which employ all kinds of materials, from blossoms to dried gourds and feathers, to create authentic tributes to the natural world. Although often irascible and bad-tempered, Burle Marx was an entertainer of the first order, and gave legendary parties, during which he was inclined to break into an aria and delight his guests with his wonderful singing voice.

Feasts of Fish

After visiting the worlds of two powerful exponents of the beauties of Brazil, you may need some lunch. Fish is on the menu; indeed you probably won't have seen so many fish restaurants in a row anywhere in the world. There are two of special interest, though both become very crowded on weekends. The first is **Tia Palmira** (Caminho do Souza 18; tel: 2410-

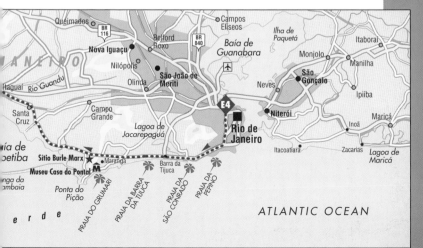

0549; Tues–Sun), half-way up a sinuous lane leading out of the main square in Guaratiba. There are no worries about what to choose here, as the friendly staff just keep bringing you fishy things until you can eat no more. The setting is simplicity itself, the roof pierced by a magnificent *siriguela* tree, whose scarlet fruit ripen in the summer. You can expect to pay about US$20 per person, without drinks, for all you can eat.

The second recommended place for lunch is **Bira de Guaratiba** (Estrada da Vendinha 68A; tel: 2410-8304; Thur–Sun), on the road back towards the Sítio Burle Marx. It is also up a steep slope and practically impossible to find on your own; your cab driver should know it, but if not, don't be afraid to ask. Bira is Tia Palmira's son, but they are not rivals in any sense. Bira offers select *à la carte* fish dishes to a demanding fan club of local people on a plant-laden veranda with gorgeous views. You are expected to share a dish here, as portions are so enormous: more shrimp than most people can consume will cost about US$30. At the time of writing, Bira does not accept credit cards, but you could call to check if this has changed when you visit.

Praia do Grumari and Prainha

Before heading back to Rio, there remains one more delight on this trip: ask your cab driver to take the turning off the Estrada de Guaratiba to the right for Grumari and Prainha. You go over a hill, where the undergrowth is fighting for road space with the very sparse traffic, winding up and then down, to emerge on glorious **Praia do Grumari**, framed by dense vegetation. Next comes **Praia do Prainha**, and in between these two beaches is a stunning view that will remain with you long after memories of other experiences in Rio have faded.

2. DAY TOUR TO PETROPOLIS *(see pullout map)*

A day tour to one of Rio's favorite retreats, founded by Dom Pedro II in the mid-19th century as a place to escape to in summer.

The road connecting Rio to Petrópolis and the hills is a good one, and well-signposted, but a car is rather a nuisance in the busy historic center of Petrópolis, and the bus service from the Rodoviária Novo Rio terminal is punctual and comfortable. The Rio–Petrópolis buses depart on the hour and the half-hour, the trip takes 1 hour 20 minutes, and the fare is approximately US$8.

The bus terminal in Petrópolis is a bustling place, with lots of shouting and an all-pervasive smell of frying from the cauldrons of boiling oil in which most Brazilian snacks are prepared. Aim for the tourist information booth and pick up the latest brochures and restaurant suggestions. As you would expect from one of the most-visited sites on the Brazilian tourist circuit, there are plenty of restaurants of all kinds. You could buy your return ticket to Rio at this stage, but do allow at least three hours in order to do this outing justice – more if you want to have lunch there. On the way up you should try for a seat on the left as you face the driver. As you climb into the hills, vegetation becomes more dense, the clouds seem closer, the granite mountains more solid.

Touring the Town

Once in Petrópolis, it makes sense to hire a cab for the hilly part of the visit, which takes in two interesting destinations. Thereafter, all the attractions are within easy walking distance of each other. Petrópolis is a seriously one-way city, so you seem to be going around in circles most of the time; this can't be helped, and indeed should be enjoyed. Beautiful homes and well-tended gardens line the avenues, and an aura of grandeur pervades. This grandeur harks back to the middle of the 19th century when the entire Brazilian court, government and diplomatic representatives moved to Petrópolis in the emperor's wake to sit out the sweltering summers in comfort.

Ask the cab driver to take you to the **Trono de Fátima** (Fatima's Throne; daily 8.30am–6pm; free) and wait for you. As you start to wind up the hill to the Fátima lookout, you will pass the Catholic University on your right, with its pretty floral clock. When you get to the top of the hill, you may wonder whether it was worth the visit, as the actual monument is modest at best. The views, however, are what you have really come for. They are far from modest, and from this vantage point you can appreciate how Petrópolis, the fourth-largest commercial center in the state of Rio de Janeiro,

Above Left: mending nets. **Left:** Bira de Guaratiba. **Right** the view from Fatima's Throne

has grown sinuously around the river that traverses it, and how completely integrated it is with the surrounding forest.

Father of Aviation

Your next stop is the **Casa de Santos Dumont** (Tues–Sun 9.30am–5.30pm; small admission charge), where you can discharge the cab. The question

of who was the first man to fly still generates controversy in some circles, but you are in Brazil, so forget about the Wright brothers. Alberto Santos Dumont, the Father of Aviation, was a native of Rio's neighboring state of Minas Gerais, and is locally revered. His youthful career as an inventor took place mainly in Paris, where he made the first fully documented flight in 1906 (the Wright brothers' flight was three years earlier, but lacked documentation at the time). By 1918, Santos Dumont was back in Brazil, seriously depressed by the use to which aviation was being put in World War I, and a confirmed, if very practical, eccentric.

His eccentricities are evident in some features of the summer residence he built here, starting with the steps. Obsessively superstitious, he believed that nothing could go well if it were not approached with one's right foot. Consequently, the steps to his home are built in such a way that it is impossible to ascend them using the left foot first. Simplicity itself, the house has great charm. Bed and desk are one and the same, built into the wall of the tiny upstairs room. The shower shows his inventiveness: an alcohol heater warms water, which is then channeled through an up-ended, perforated tin bucket. In the roof he installed his telescope, all the better to observe his beloved skies.

Royal Resting Place

Leaving the chalet-style house behind you will see, straight ahead, soaring above the river and its red bridges, the 70-m (230-ft) spire of the **Catedral de São Pedro de Alcântara** (Tues–Sun 8am–noon, 2–6pm; free). Although commissioned in 1843, the same year as the founding of Petrópolis, the cathedral underwent serious financial set-backs and was not opened till 1929. Actual completion of the building only took place 40 years after that. Neo-Gothic touches dominate a mixture of architectural styles, and the cathedral has a noble feel, with the daylight penetrating the stained-glass windows. Above it all is the image of St Peter, in Carrara marble, bronze and onyx. This is the final burial place of Dom Pedro II and Dona Teresa Cristina. Their remains were returned to Pedro's beloved Petrópolis in 1939, as the law banishing the royal family, dead or alive, had been revoked in 1920. Pedro's daughter, Isabel, and her French husband, the Count D'Eu, were also buried here, but not until 1971.

Above: stained-glass windows in the cathedral

A Gem of a Museum

With the cathedral behind you, a pleasant walk to the left leads to the town's prime attraction, the **Museu Imperial** (tel: 24-2237-8000; Tues–Sun 11am–5.30pm; admission charge). There will be a line of horse-drawn buggies here, ready to take visitors for a ride; there is no more delightful way to tour the historic center of Petrópolis, and you could do so now, before visiting the museum. When you get back from your jaunt, your first task within the museum will be to don the felt overshoes handed to you when you buy your ticket – wearing these, you both protect and polish the floors as you go along. Don't try any acrobatics in them, as the floors are buffed sheer. An

audio-guide, which will talk you through the palace, is available, at an extra cost. In the marbled foyer, you will be asked to leave your bags and cameras in a locked cupboard, to which you keep the key. The museum shop is at the end of the tour, so you may want to keep some cash on you to spend on gifts or souvenirs.

Realistically set out as the summer residence it once was, every room in the museum contains something of interest. The dining room seems only to await the arrival of the guests for the meal to start. In the sewing room you can almost hear the chatter of the court ladies, and admire the neatness of the japanned and ivory

Above: a leisurely form of transport
Right: slippers on in the Museu Imperial

sewing box. The delightful music room, with views over the lawn, was inaugurated in 1852 on Dom Pedro II's 26th birthday. Pedro's interest in matters scientific is evident from the paraphernalia in his study.

The jewels exert their own fascination, shining brightly in their dimly lit cabinets. Up the stairs – remove the overshoes for this section – domesticity takes over. The beds look small and hard, the facilities very basic, and the babies' cribs look positively terrifying, but in spite of this, the house would undeniably be a great place to spend the summer months. Take time to examine the exhibits in detail for a delightful visit to the recent past. When you think you have done the main part of the museum justice, remember to retrieve your belongings from the foyer; relief from the overshoes is just a marble hall away.

Transport and Lunch

Turning right into the patio, make your way to the carriage house. Various forms of transport and traction are represented here, evoking the days of silent traffic and gently jogging journeys. A locomotive of the Leopoldina line is parked on mock rails opposite, setting the scene for a pleasant place to relax and put your feet up. Alternatively, you could wander back down the main driveway and, when you have almost reached the exit, you will see a doll's house-like structure to your right. This is the Petit Palais, a peaceful place to have a gourmet sandwich or a full meal, reasonably priced and in the best possible taste.

It may now be time to find your way back to the bus station. Turn left as you leave the museum, past the horse-drawn buggies. Keep going for some 10 minutes, and you will find yourself in the middle of a muddle of traffic and hundreds of shoppers on the streets. Cross over the river to the far sidewalk, and follow signs for the Rodoviária. Back down the hill you go, to sea level and the modern world.

Above: the splendid façade of the Museu Imperial

3. PAQUETA ISLAND AND GUANABARA BAY
(see map, page 52)

A trip across the Bay of Guanabara to a flower-filled, vehicle-free island that has inspired novelists, poets and painters.

Start from the ferry station in Praça Quinze, in the heart of downtown Rio. Paquetá is reached either by conventional ferries (barcas) *or by modern hydrofoils* (aerobarcos). *It makes sense to go across at the leisurely pace of the ferry (tickets cost under US$1) and return by hydrofoil (less than US$3). On weekdays, ferries depart at 10.30am and 1.30pm; the return trip can be made on hydrofoils from Paquetá at 2.30pm or 4.30pm. On the ferry, the trip takes just over an hour; on the hydrofoil, about 20 minutes.*

While the sophisticated section of Rio society snootily turns its nose up at **Paquetá**, this is where local people go with their families for a fun and inexpensive day out. The pace is sleepy, the crime rate negligible and the

natives extremely friendly: this outing may provide a welcome break if the traffic and frantic activity of Rio become too much for you. But Paquetá, for all its natural charms, is something of a gastronomic wasteland, so bring your own food; if your hotel does picnic lunches this would be a good time to order one. Alternatively, you can get snacks at a variety of bars and basic eateries. Pick a clear day for this jaunt, and do not undertake it on a sunny summer weekend, as the island can become very crowded.

The **Praça Quinze ferry station** is rundown and somewhat daunting, but ticketing is efficient. There are no numbered seats on the ferries, so take your pick. Upstairs is rowdy and fun, downstairs much quieter. The views are great from either deck, and you are free to wander around. The capacity is a staggering 2,000 passengers, minded by eight crew members. There are facilities, but don't expect the Ritz. Vendors of food, drink or souvenirs are forbidden, but they do occasionally creep on board to sell their wares.

Rio in Perspective

As you pull away from the dock and the huge ferry does a U-turn, downtown Rio takes on quite a different perspective, dominated by the ultramodern, triangular tower of an office block at Praça Mauá. To starboard is the runway of Santos Dumont airport, which services the Rio–São Paulo route. To the port side is the strange, greenish neo-Gothic building on **Ilha Fiscal** that hosted the last grand ball of the empire in 1889, shortly before the fall of the monarchy. The backdrop is the dramatic **Serra dos Orgãos** (Organ Mountain Range), supposedly named for its resemblance to the pipes of an organ, though you would be forgiven for thinking the name is more anatomical in origin. Everywhere around you is evidence of Rio's rank as one of the world's busiest ports, with vessels in every stage of repair all over the bay.

Some 20 minutes after departure from Praça Quinze, the ferry goes under the dramatic **Rio–Niterói Bridge**. At this stage you begin to appreciate why the first European visitors, 500 years ago, thought the bay was the mouth of a river, and therefore gave it the name River of January (the month they arrived). To port is the Ilha do Governador, home to the international airport, and beyond, the industrial areas.

Around the Island

Arrival on the island of Paquetá is a noisy affair, as the crowds of local guides jostle for the most promising-looking visitors. You can't buy your ticket to return to Rio at this stage because there are no advance tickets sales. Pick up some maps and leaflets at the tourist information booth straight ahead of you. To get a feel for the place, start with a horse-drawn buggy ride (you will notice a strong smell of horse when you disembark). You hire a buggy for either an hour or half an hour; prices are low, and regulated by the authorities. The trip may help you decide which beach you want to return to under your own steam, or where you want to spend a quiet interlude before returning to Rio.

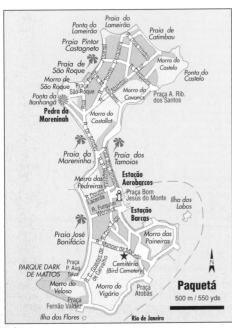

All around you are well-kept gardens, with plants flourishing in this exhaust-free area. Striking flamboyant trees (otherwise known as royal poincianas) drip tangerine-colored flowers during the summer.

Itineraries may vary slightly according to the condition of the unpaved roads, the whim of the buggy driver or even the mood of the horse. The route taken is bound to include an early stop at a strange memorial in highly questionable taste, the bird cemetery. Then your driver will probably take you to the **Praia José Bonifácio**, the island's busiest beach, with vendors of coconuts and snacks, and boats and canoes for hire. To your left as you

Above: taking a break in the shade
Right: Paquetá's pretty church

face the water is the Parque Darke de Mattos, which offers great views. Onwards to **Praia da Moreninha**, the setting for the eponymous novel written by Joaquim Manuel de Macedo in the mid-18th century. From here you can climb to the top of the **Pedra da Moreninha** for outstanding views. The palatial structure in front of you is the Palacio de Brocoió, one of the official residences of Rio's authorities. Around the point you reach the **Praia de São Roque**, much frequented by fishermen. The next beach is muddy **Praia do Lameirão**, which is no good for swimming, but great for catching crabs. At the northernmost point of the island is **Praia de Catimbau**, with splendid views of the Organ Mountain Range, and the newly restored, distant mangrove swamps of Guapimirim in the distance.

Praia dos Tamoios

All roads lead eventually to **Praia dos Tamoios**, named for the indigenous people who first lived here. This is a residential, as opposed to tourist, beach, but holds two points of interest for the visitor. Opposite house No. 425 is a rare and extremely old baobob tree, sacred in parts of Africa, with a circumference of 7m (23ft). The tree is protected by a preservation order, and known to local people as *Maria Gorda* (Fat Mary). In the middle of the road, opposite house No. 341, is the last remaining cannon, which was used to hail the arrival of Pedro II, who visited Paquetá frequently in the early 1800s and used to call the place the Island of Love.

This is where your buggy ride comes to an end. What you do with the rest of your time on the island depends on your tastes. A good option is to hire one of the various forms of bicycle available, return to a beach for a swim, and do some investigating on your own.

Hydrofoils depart for Rio from the Praia dos Tamoios, and the embarkation point is just to the north of the ferry station where you arrived. Tickets go on sale about half an hour before departure. Try for a seat towards the front of the boat, as those to the rear are low and provide no views. There is none of the romance of the ferry boat here, just a noisy trip at high speed which takes you back into the heart of busy downtown Rio in a mere 20 minutes.

4. PARATY AND THE GREEN COAST *(see pullout map)*

This excursion takes you through a paradise such as you may have thought no longer existed. Walking, climbing, swimming, diving, boating, shopping – it's all here. To make it worthwhile, you need to spend one night away from Rio; to do it justice, you could stay forever.

The distance from Rio to Paraty is some 236km (163 miles). If traveling by car, note that the road surface can be a little challenging, and you do not want to be on the road at night or during weekend rushes, when traffic can slow to a standstill. If traveling by bus, many regular lines, including the Costa Verde line (tel: 2516-2437), from Rio's long-haul bus terminus, Rodoviária (tel: 2291-5151), allow for a degree of flexibility in planning.

Leaving Rio

Rio's **Costa Verde** (Green Coast) is an absolute wonderland for visitors. The Rio–Santos highway hugs the coastline, unveiling spectacular views of picture-book beaches, rocky shorelines and majestic mountains. From a driver's point of view, the highway is serviceable and well-signposted; avoid

the odd crater that might open up before you, and beware of landslides during summer. Orientation is simple: keep the mountains on your right and the sea on your left. As some of the beaches are sheltered from the open sea by spits and islands, not all are clean; others are unreachable, as access is restricted to the owners of luxury villas in gated communities; others are off limits as they are enclosed within nature reserves. But with several hundred to choose from, there are still plenty left over. We shall concentrate on some easy-to-manage destinations – Itacuruçá, Angra dos Reis, Ilha Grande and Paraty.

If you have rented a car, get out of Rio by aiming for Leblon, São Conrado and the interminable district of Barra da Tijuca. Some of Rio's worst driving takes place along Barra's main street, the Avenida das Américas, so it will be a relief when you start to climb a small hill at the end and leave the chaos behind. Views are lovely: behind you, the densely occupied Barra district, seemingly in perpetual motion, before you, fields of nothing, penned between the sea and the mountains. Your target is Santa Cruz. This is a shocker of a dormitory town with horse-drawn carts vying with powerful trucks for road space, and street vendors' loud hailers producing a nightmarish din. Cross the railway bridge, and aim for Angra dos Reis, still on the Rio–Santos highway. Soon you will be on the open road, experiencing some of the most magnificent scenery the tropical world has to offer.

Tropical Island Tour

Although you are following the signs for Angra dos Reis, there are many stopping places on the way. **Itacuruçá** is one, a sleepy village, where the pace of life is tranquil. This is the port from which the Tropical Island Tours

depart *(see Practical Information, page 91)*. This is a traditional Rio visitor attraction, and can be reserved as a day tour directly from your hotel. The town jolts awake as the huge tourist buses rumble in to deposit their passengers on the quayside, ready for a four-hour cruise around the islands, which includes a stop for lunch and several for swimming. Throughout this whole area, mosquitoes can be a real menace, so take plenty of repellent.

The next town of any importance is **Mangaratiba**, busier than Itacuruçá, but again offering only basic infrastructure for foreign visitors. A daily ferry connects Mangaratiba with the stunning scenery and clear beaches of Ilha Grande, the destination of choice for many people. The only snag is that the ferry leaves Mangaratiba at 8am, so is extremely difficult to catch if you are starting your day in Rio. However, there are plenty of local boats for hire here, and you can make an arrangement with a boatman either to cruise around the area or to take you to Ilha Grande.

Angra dos Reis and Ilha da Gipóia

Onwards to **Angra dos Reis** (King's Cove), a misnomer if ever there was one. Today's kings of industry, commerce, and cash merely call in to the busy, unattractive town to pick up supplies for consumption at their mansions or to take on their luxury cruisers to private islands. If traveling by bus, the station is approximately 1km (less than a mile) from the hub of things, which is at the main quayside. No distance from the bus station, in the opposite direction to the town, is the monstrous Pirata's Mall, with a supermarket, fast-food outlets, and lots of boats for hire. This is not worth a detour. Instead, take a cab or any bus saying 'Circular' into the town. The only reason (but a good one) to come to Angra is to take a boat trip, and a huge variety of local vessels, large and small, are lined up ready to take you to Ilha Grande or for a cruise around the magazine-cover bays. The boats belong to the Associação de Barqueiros de Angra dos Reis (Angra Boatmen's Association), which consists of 60 members, many of whom have inherited membership from their fathers and grandfathers. The association's boats are regularly

Above: there are stunning beaches all the way along the coast

inspected for seaworthiness, and are equipped with lifejackets and emergency equipment. The boatmen have a published price list – approximately US$10 an hour, or US$100 a day for a boat that carries from one to 10 people – but these prices are very much open to negotiation, so haggle like mad – it's expected. If you want to make an advance reservation, the phone number is tel: (24) 3365-3165, but if you just turn up at the dockside you are bound to find plenty of boats on offer.

The **Ilha da Gipóia** is a natural destination, some 20 minutes by boat from downtown Angra. Praia Jurubaíba is the headquarters for party people, with its narrow sands and calm waters. On weekends, improvized bars float around, providing the many visitors with drinks and snacks. If bigger waves and reefs are what you are looking for, Praia Sururu is for you. Praia Piedade is where the fishermen congregate, and you can visit the ruins of an old farmhouse and a curious peninsula connected to the mainland by a mere spit.

Ilha Grande

Ilha Grande offers a huge range of scenic, outdoor experiences. Originally a holding pen for the slave trade, it then became a haven for pirates. More recently, Ilha Grande was home to one of the country's most notorious jails, which was imploded, to widespread relief, in 1994. Two nature reserves occupy much of the island, and steps are being taken to ensure it retains its natural characteristics and beauty.

Ilha Grande is served by a regular ferry service, which takes you from Angra dos Reis to the little town of Vila do Abraão for approximately US$1.50. The trip takes about 80 minutes and during the week the daily departure is at 3.30pm. On weekends and public holidays, the fare rises to about US$4, and the ferry leaves at 1.30pm. The return trip departs from

Abraão at 10am, which obviously means you have to spend the night on the island. This should present no hardship, as there are plentiful bed-and-breakfast establishments, ranging from the most basic to the extremely chic. However, if time is of the essence and you cannot spend the night on the island, tailor your own trip by using the services of the Angra Boatmen's Association *(see previous page)*.

The many wonderful beaches are separated by trails through breathtaking countryside, offering spectacular views. Some trails are quite a test of feet and fitness; a less arduous way to see the island is to hire a boat and visit the beaches from the water. The Saco do Céu, some 6km (4 miles) by sea from Abraão, is picture-postcard material, surrounded by mangroves and framed by mountains. A further 27km (17 miles) westwards is Praia Ubatubinha, with a quayside and clear waters, perfect for diving. A trail connects it to the tiny Praia Tapera and Praia Sítio Forte. Proceeding counter-clockwise around the island, Praia Provetá is 500m/yds long with thick yellow sand, and is sheltered in a jewel of a bay. At the southernmost point of the island is Praia dos Meros, which faces the open sea, and is an excellent place for diving. Tradition has it that a dragon inhabited Praia Ponta do Drago, killing all the fishermen; a priest was called in to exorcise the spot and the dragon met a watery end. Praia Parnaioca is well known for its fishing, and the lake and small waterfall formed by the estuary of the Parnaioca River add interest, as does the wreck of a sunken cargo ship off the point. Praia Lopes Mendes, 3km (2 miles) long and traversed by three rivers, has crystal clear waters. One could spend a week on Ilha Grande and not scratch the surface of what it has to offer.

Eventually it will be time to head back to the mainland. On arrival at Angra, make for the bus station where you rarely have to wait more than an hour for the Paraty bus. The trip takes two hours, and costs about US$2. If you are driving yourself, go back to the Rio–Santos highway, heading west and encircling the spectacular bay of Angra, for approximately 100km (60 miles).

Paraty

What is it about **Paraty**? Reams have been written about it, but you need to be there to experience the amalgam of old and new, seascapes and tropical rainforest, visitors in search of a good time, and the laid-back local population. Get your bearings, and a map, at the excellent tourist information center at the corner of Rua Roberto da Silveira and Rua Domingos Gonçalves de Abreu, on the boundary of old and new Paraty. The trip back to Rio takes some four hours, so you may decide to spend the night. Dozens of bed-and-breakfasts offer every level of comfort at reasonable prices. Ensure you get a room with air-conditioning during the summer months, as the heat can be overpowering.

Above Left: painting a local scene. **Left:** a sheltered Costa Verde bay
Above Right: ferries from Itacuruça take visitors on tours of the islands

While outer Paraty has nothing much to recommend it, inner Paraty is a jewel. The historic city center is cordoned off by massive chains, which do the job of keeping the modern world at bay, physically and psychologically. No cars are allowed in the city center, but the decent guesthouses all have lock-up garages within walking distance. Getting around on foot poses its own minor problems, as the flagstone paving is irregular.

Paraty is one of the few tidal towns in the area and when the tide is in, entire streets are cut off by water. Legend has it that this seeming failure to take account of the effects of nature when drawing up the town plan in the 1600s was intentional; the tide washes the low-lying streets clean of the detritus of civilization. Much has been written about the original planning of the town, including the Masonic influence, which pitches corners and intersections at seemingly unnatural angles.

Bric-à-brac and Booze

Artists of all types are drawn by the magnetism of Paraty, and almost every house in the historic center is open to the public as a shop or showroom. Tile painters, weavers, decorators of knick-knacks, builders of miniature ships – you name it, it's there. But if you ask Brazilians what Paraty is famous for, the answer will be unanimous: booze. Not just ordinary

booze, but *cachaça*, the fiery brew produced from sugar cane. Several operators will take you on a tour of a distillery, where even to breathe too deeply is to risk immediate inebriation. The most famous of the distilleries is **Fazenda Murycana** (daily 10am–6pm; minimal admission charge), 5km (3 miles) out of town on the road to Cunha. It houses a museum and restaurant, and offers lovely walks through the Bocaina National Park.

Casa de Cultura

Paraty and its people have a great sense of identity, and this is nowhere better displayed than in the stunning **Casa de Cultura** (Sun–Mon and Wed–Thur 10am–6.30pm, Fri–Sat 1–9.30pm; minimal admission charge), at the intersection of Rua Dona Geralda and Rua Samuel Costa. This is a monument to Paraty, and to its people, their simplicity and dignity. On the ground floor are a bookshop, souvenir shop and café; upstairs is a permanent exhibition that is vibrant, full of personality and visually astonishing.

Above: knick-knacks for sale in Paraty. **Left:** a door in Paraty's characterful old town
Right: night in Paraty

The Gold Trail

A recent and highly successful initiative has re-traced the routes taken by the gold prospectors of the 1700s from the mines in Minas Gerais to the port of Paraty. This has provided yet another leisure option in the area, one that combines history, nature, adventure and some fabulous scenery. Especially adapted open trucks take visitors to the village of **Penha**. From here there is a 2.5km (1½-mile) hike, accompanied by a most useful creature, the *frigo-burro* (cooler-donkey). This innovative beast of burden carries iced drinks for refreshment along the way. On arrival at the historical farmhouse, lunch awaits, as well as any number of outdoor activities, including just sitting around soaking up the historic surroundings. Departures are from the Teatro Espaço at Rua Dona Geralda 327 in the old town of Paraty (Wednesday–Sunday at 10am, returning by 4 or 5pm). Further information can be had on tel: (24) 3371-1575. The cost of the outing is approximately US$10, with a further US$5 for lunch. Other guides who specialize in the Gold Trail can be contacted at the Sebrae office, at Avenida Roberto da Silveira, tel: (24) 3371-1783, just outside the old town boundary.

Food and Fun

With new bars and restaurants springing up all the time in Paraty, the atmosphere is quite bohemian. The Porto restaurant at Rua do Comércio 36 has been acclaimed by such as the *Condé Nast Traveler*, and is pricey and stylish. The stalwart Restaurante do Hiltinho has been serving good meals at Rua Marechal Deodoro 233 for many years; they now have a branch on the Ilha do Algodão, as well as running their own schooner tours.

Paraty's calendar is filled with festivities – religious, literary, and gastronomic. The major religious festival is that of the Divine Holy Spirit, which is a moveable feast, but usually held around the end of May. The now internationally famous literary festival, FLIP (Festa Literária de Parati) takes place early in July, when the town simply hums with celebrities and upheaval. At all other times of the year, you should be able to take your pick of places to stay. Enjoy Paraty, the environment, the people, the light, and the tides. It may well be the high point of your trip to this part of the world.

5. BUZIOS *(see pullout map)*

An excursion to a beautiful place where pleasure-seekers hold parties in an idyllic seaside setting. To offset the air of hedonism, adventure sports and healthy outdoor activities can be enjoyed within easy reach of the resort. Plan to stay overnight, or longer *(see pages 64–5)*.

Reaching Búzios from Rio is easy, provided you avoid the mass exodus on long weekends. The Viação 1001 company runs an inexpensive and reliable service from the Rodoviária (tel: 2291-5151), Rio's long-haul bus terminus in the dock area. The journey takes three hours, with a strategic relief stop. Buses leave Rio at two-hourly intervals between 6.30am and 7.30pm. For the return journey, the first bus departs from Búzios at 7am, the last at 7pm. Check exact times by calling the bus company (tel: 2625-1001 and 2625-0577). If getting the evening bus back, bear in mind that the Rodoviária is an unsavory place to be at night. Alternatively, this may be the time to rent a car and meander eastwards on your own.

The potential of **Armação de Búzios** as a fishing port was discovered by a Portuguese trader way back in 1760. Whales as well as fish were processed on this out-of-the-way peninsula, miles from anywhere. Today, there is not much left in the waters to fish, but Búzios fishermen continue out of an historic sense of duty. Today, the main industry in Búzios is catering to sun-loving, pleasure-seeking visitors. Blame it all on Brigitte Bardot, sulky star of the sixties, who 'discovered' the peninsula back in 1964. The French screen star, sex goddess, and (later) animal-rights campaigner, put the place on the international map. People who have been coming here for years will tell you that Búzios has gone to the dogs, that property speculation has blotted its beautiful horizons and

Above: by the salt flats on the way to Búzios
Left: a monument in memory of the slave colony at Rasa

that the infrastructure is overburdened by the demands of thousands of visitors. They may well be right, but Búzios is still well worth a visit, not only for what is has been, but for what it still is: a peek into paradise.

On the Way to Paradise

If you have decided to go under your own steam, aim for the Rio–Niterói Bridge, remembering that you will have to pay a small toll to cross it, and follow signs for Rio Bonito and Região dos Lagos. Make for the Via Lagos, a toll highway, and keep following signs for Região dos Lagos and, specifically, Búzios. Bear in mind that the official name is Armação de Búzios, which is what some of the signs say, just to confuse matters. If getting out of Rio under your own steam seems too daunting, then get the bus and rent a vehicle when you get there – a beach buggy is fun.

However you choose to travel, once you leave the chaos of Rio's outskirts, the green pastures that flank the road will be a welcome relief. The cows you see grazing, grayish-white in color and with a pronounced hump on their shoulders, are of the hardy Zebu breed, which was introduced into Brazil from India in 1870 for haulage work on the coffee plantations. Take another look at that hump: you may well come across it again in a somewhat different form in a *churrascaria* (barbecue restaurant), under the name of *cupim*, packed with cholesterol and oh-so-tender.

Banana trees wave their ungainly arms as you pass; stately avenues of palms indicate homesteads of grandeur, past or present. Evidence of the success of brick-making in the area can still be seen in the number of chimneys reaching for the sky. Roadside commerce thrives, especially on weekends and in the high season. Here you can see the output of many kilns: flower pots of every shape, size and garish color; Snow White and the seven dwarfs; improbable clay zebras; smiling dolphins; haughty egrets and frolicking frogs. In better taste are the freshly picked manioc and okra, bunches of finger-sized bananas, cashew fruit and the ubiquitous coconuts. Somewhat strangely, stalls selling earthenware cooking pots, *panelas de barro*, outnumber all the others. They are ludicrously cheap, so one can only assume they are not built to last.

Reaching your Destination

You know you are nearly at Búzios when you reach a traffic circle on an incline, in the middle of which stands a sculpted slave offering his child to the skies. This is a tribute to the slave colony that used to be at Rasa, the first beach you will see as you crest the hill and find your way to the sea. Praia Rasa (Shallow Beach), is a somewhat hostile length of sand with casuarina trees bowing to the strength of the unremitting wind. The road veers away from the beach, and your next landmark is the Búzios Portico, which houses

Right: get your garden ornaments along the road to Búzios

the tourist information center. Carry on down the main street and you will reach the narrowest part of the peninsula, with the famous **Praia Geribá** on your right, and Praia Manguinhos on your left. Continue through the crowded main street to downtown Búzios. If you have traveled by bus, there will be no problem about when to get off: when the bus parks, you know you've reached your destination.

Trolley Tours

There's no better way to get your bearings than by taking the **Búzios Trolley** on Praia da Armação (tel: [22] 2623-2763 and [22] 2623-4733). Especially adapted trucks can carry 35 passengers per trip, protected from the sun by a canopy but open at the sides to the cooling breezes. Regardless of the number of passengers, the tours leave at 9am, noon, and 3pm. Over a two-hour period, they give an overview of Búzios, its neighborhoods and it beaches – in all, you visit 12 of them – all with their different characteristics. The tour costs about US$15, which includes fresh fruit, soft drinks, and snacks, all dispensed as you travel along. If you're early for the trolley, you can have a quick nine holes at the mini-golf range while you wait.

The tour starts on Orla Bardot, the seaside road and path named in honor of Búzios illustrious 1960s visitor; there is even a statue of her, sitting patiently on her battered suitcase, gazing out to sea. Your next landmark is the Yacht Club and port area, where massive cruise ships dock and disgorge hundreds of visitors throughout the season. The fishing origins of the village are commemorated here with a clever *trompe l'oeil* group of sculpted fishermen eternally hauling in their catch: their hats provide a great perch for the frigate birds. Next, you head off in the direction of the northernmost point of the peninsula, toward Praia João Fernandes. Sumptuous summer homes line the roads, and the occasional windsock indicates that some of the home-owners are true high flyers, using helicopters to beat the traffic out of town. Doubling back on itself the trolley climbs up to a look-out spot, high above Praia Brava. The next stop reveals the stunning views of Praia do Forno

and Praia da Foca. Southwards, the trip takes you to the ever-popular **Praia Ferradura** (Horseshoe Beach).

The Búzios Trolley company also runs a full-service agency organizing visits to local attractions; as does Mister Tour at Rua das Pedras 21 (tel: [22] 2623-2100 or [22] 2623-1022).

Where the Action Is

As you will have seen from your reconnaisance trip on the trolley, **Rua das Pedras** is the nub of the matter, where all the action is. This central area of Búzios has been pedestrianized, but distances are not great and there is plenty to see and do as you wander around. Vestiges of the old fishing village hide behind eye-catching shop windows. Famous-name brands from Rio and São Paulo have outlets here, and the pace of life is conducive to browsing and shopping. Many of the shops are closed in the morning, but stay open until the wee hours. At night, the vendors take over the streets, which are

lined with carts preparing fruity cock- tails – quite delicious, and guaranteed to put a spring in your step – or give you an instant hangover. You can have braids put in your hair, tattoos applied to your body, or your fortune told, all to the beat of loud music emanating from the bars.

A traditional meeting and hanging- out point is Chez Michou (Rua das Pedras 90), an informal crêperie that has broken records for restaurant longevity in Búzios, and still serves countless inexpensive crêpes every day. More upmarket is Brigitta's, a 1930s fisherman's cottage converted into a colorful bar, restaurant, and guesthouse. The Pátio Havana, which is on the expensive side, overlooks the sea and oozes style. Still on Rua das Pedras is the Cigalon, where you can enjoy sophisticated French cuisine only steps away from the beach. If you hanker for Mexican food, call in at Guapo Loco, for *tacos, quesadillas* and *burritos*. Value for money, good food and a happy atmosphere are on offer at the help-yourself-and-weigh-your-plate establishment called Boom, which is on Rua Manuel T. de Freitas, parallel to Rua das Pedras. Back towards the headquarters of the trolley is the multi-purpose Privilège, with a heav- ing dance floor, sushi bar, lounge, terrace, café and international cuisine. In between are any number of bars and restaurants; there's no danger of going hungry, much less thirsty, in Búzios. Just follow your nose, and mind your step: the paving stones are not kind to your feet.

Hotels and Habits

The vacation high season officially runs from December through March, when Búzios becomes very crowded indeed. Prices for accommodations are con- siderably higher at this time, and high-season prices are also charged on

Left: outside Chez Michou restaurant, which has broken records for longevity
Above Right: hot, hot, hot on a market stall in Búzios

any long weekend or national holiday, so make sure you know what you are paying before you bed down for the night.

There are literally hundreds of places to stay, from huge resorts to small bed-and-breakfast establishments. At the top end of the market are the full-service hotels, such as La Bohème, with its great views of João Fernandes beach. Then there's the lovely Casas Brancas, convenient for downtown. Geribá beach is a popular destination, though it can get crowded. At the lower end of the scale, you will find simple, owner-managed guesthouses, providing the basics plus breakfast, but not much more. Appearances can be deceptive, so do your research. Búzios is a fairly fickle market, dependent on some unexpected factors, and the survival rate of smaller guesthouses and restaurants is not high.

Búzios is hot, although you can usually count on a breeze. It is also extremely casual, so you need not take your party gear. Just pack shorts and T-shirts, sunscreen and a hat, and you're in business. People keep strange hours in Búzios. If you are one of nature's larks you may be lonely, as virtually nothing happens until after 11am. Owls will feel more at home, as things pick up in the early evening and keep going throughout the noisy night.

Excursions from Búzios

Apart from beach-hopping in water taxis and generally soaking up the sun, there are plenty of fun excursions to be made from Búzios. It makes sense to use one of the professional tour operators *(see pages 90–91)*, who know the ropes and take the guesswork and possible errors out of things – always useful when time is limited.

Cabo Frio is the nearest large town, and quite missable, but **Arraial do Cabo**, some 30 minutes by car from Búzios, is worth a visit for its crystal clear, greenish-blue waters, which make it a must for divers. The views from the Pontal do Atalaia are especially spectacular. **Sana** and **Casemiro de Abreu** are both within easy distance of Búzios; both places have incredible scenery and some of the best the natural world has to offer in terms of leisure activities. White-water rafting, abseiling, country walks, horseback riding and showering in waterfalls all offer a pure adrenaline rush in fairytale surroundings.

Closer to Búzios, the **Praia Olho de Boi** (Bull's Eye Beach) is the place for those who feel overdressed in a fig leaf: this tiny beach, which is accessible only on foot from Praia Brava on the northeastern coast of the peninsula, is an official nudist beach.

Above: fishing boat, Armação beach
Right: Praia Barra, Rio's longest beach

6. THE BEST BEACHES *(see pullout map)*

This is not an itinerary in itself, but a run-down of the best beaches in and around Rio, the wonderful stretches of sand that are, for some, one of the city's main attractions.

Traffic is banned from eastbound lanes of the beach road on Sunday, turning the entire shoreline into a giant playground for walkers, joggers, skaters and cyclists. Serious sun worshipers will enjoy the beaches in the Paraty and Búzios excursions (see pages 55 and 61).

Beach Behavior

Unfortunately, a significant portion of Rio's petty crime takes place along the beaches, so take nothing with you that you are not prepared to part with, and only enough cash to buy the food and drink you will consume while you are there. Leave your camera behind: it is worth returning to a particular spot for the sole purpose of photographing it. Beach thieves, often children, are cunning and creative so let caution be your watchword at all times. Some of the major beachfront hotels have 'colonised' their stretches of beach and provide security guards, deckchairs and bar facilities.

Remember that the sun is fierce, and a bad case of sunburn could ruin your vacation. Protect yourself with sunscreen, a hat, and a garment with long sleeves. Drink plenty of non-alcoholic beverages to avoid dehydration. Best of all is coconut water, full of potassium and the essential minerals you will lose through perspiration. It has the advantage of being very safe to drink, coming, as it does, in nature's original packaging. Avoid consuming food and drink that looks too home-made. Stick to recognizable brands or products that show evidence of some professionalism in their preparation. Remember that mayonnaise and sunshine can be a vacation-ruining combination.

While you're here, pamper yourself and have a massage: tables are set up in shady spots and you lie there while someone else takes the knots out of your system. Bliss!

Beach Round-Up

Starting at the western end of Rio, **Praia da Barra** is Rio's longest beach, at 18km (11 miles). Some parts of the shore are built up, with bars and restaurants, others are deserted, as they form part of a nature reserve. The beach is extremely busy on weekends, but fairly quiet during the week.

Moving eastward, or toward the center of town, you come to **Praia do São Conrado**, approximately 1km (half a mile) long. At the farthest end is the famous **Praia do Pepino**, landing strip for hang-gliders. It's overlooked by the world's largest *favela* (shanty town), and the water can be filthy at times.

Praia de Leblon is for families, and they start arriving at dawn. At the corner of Rua General Venâncio Flores is the famous **Baixo Bebê**, the kiosk

where the babies of Rio are taken by their mothers or uniformed nannies for their early morning airing, and can be seen lined up in their prams.

Pit stops on this beach are limited to one bar, the **Caneco 70**, and the kiosks; try to patronize one near the funnel-shaped life-guard stations, which have restroom facilities.

Praia de Ipanema is the continuation of Leblon beach, and the most famous of all. In the morning, joggers and cyclists throng the parallel promenade, while others take their exercise on the sands. Later, it is thronged with sunbathers. Every summer a different stretch becomes the 'in' point, though the gay community's meeting point, with a rainbow flag fluttering, is fixed at the corner of Rua Farme de Amoedo. A huge bar, the **Barril 1800**, marks the spot where many stop for a beer and where Ipanema beach becomes **Praia do Arpoador**, a beach that has pedestrian-only access and is very popular with surfers.

Rounding the point, **Praia de Copacabana** is a very long stretch of beach, enlarged in the 1960s by new sand imported from Botafogo Bay. It offers every form of life and entertainment, as bars and restaurants line the shore and the kiosks are favorite gathering places. Volleyball, beach soccer, and paddle-ball are all played on this wide, sandy stretch both by adults and by school teams. If you watch a game of volleyball, you will realize why Brazil always does so well at this sport at international level; and if you watch the men working out on the gym equipment you will appeciate how seriously they take the cult of the body beautiful. At the end of Copacabana is **Praia do Leme**, which is much quieter, and more of a residents' beach.

Praia do Botafogo may look like the perfect beach, but the water is not clean. However, it is great for walking and admiring the views, with Sugar Loaf mountain dominating the scene.

Praia do Flamengo borders the **Parque do Flamengo**, a park beautifully landscaped by Roberto Burle Marx. It is close to the city center, and sports courts and paved walks make it a favorite Rio recreation area.

Above: going flat out on the beach
Right: you're never to young to go surfing on Copacabana

Leisure Activities

SHOPPING

The heady days when an unstable currency made most purchases a bargain are long gone, but Rio is still a great place to shop, whether you are looking for designer fashion, traditional crafts, jewelry or beachwear. Credit cards are widely welcomed in most shops in the malls, and in the handicraft, designer and jewelry stores elsewhere, but ensure that your particular card is acceptable before you buy. You may find that some street vendors will accept foreign currency, although there is no guarantee that you'll get a fair rate. Piracy has become a noxious feature of Brazilian retailing. You can pick up anything from CDs to designer sunglasses from street hawkers, but the goods may be falsified, and no tax has been paid on them.

The Malls

Cariocas shop all the time, and once they discovered the joys of one-stop shopping, they never looked back. Rio's air-conditioned malls, with their mix of local designer goods and international brand names, are the focus for many. Shops of all varieties, cinemas and restaurants provide the magnet, and meeting in 'the shopping' is quite the done thing. The malls are also relatively safe, compared to pounding the sidewalks of Copacabana.

Rio Sul in Botafogo is one of Rio's most beloved shopping centers, housing in excess of 400 shops and 50 restaurants (Mon–Sat 10am–10pm, Sun shops 1–9pm, restaurants and leisure sections noon–10pm). Rio Sul runs a free bus to and from many of the hotels, but it is easily reached by cab or bus.

The monster **Barra Shopping** (Mon–Sat 10am–10pm, Sun shops 3–9pm, restaurants and leisure sections daily 10am–11pm) has 546 shops, 42 restaurants and receives 2.5 million shoppers every month. The district of Barra is some way from the South Zone of Rio, and is not totally pedestrian-friendly, but really is a serious shopper's heaven.

The pocket-sized **São Conrado Fashion Mall** (Mon–Sat 10am–10pm, Sun 3–9pm), with only 157 stores, may seem more welcoming to those unused to quite so much retail choice. At the Leblon end of São Conrado beach, it caters to the top end of the market in a landscaped-garden setting. The food outlets are particularly attractive.

Handicrafts

Innate creativity and, to some degree, the lack of formal employment, ensure that almost every form of handicraft is expertly produced in Brazil. Beads, feathers, clay, stones, leather, wood are all used to produce objects for personal adornment and home decoration, as well as a variety of knick-knacks that may tempt an impulse buyer.

A shop that takes the handicraft business seriously is **Pé de Boi** at Rua Ipiranga 55 in Laranjeiras (tel: 2285-4395; Mon–Fri 9am–7pm, Sat 9am–1pm). This owner-operated store sells an impressive range of handicrafts, mainly from the northeast of the country and the state of Minas Gerais, and also carries items from other South American countries. Lacework, basketry, woodwork, feather art and ceramics produce a colorful display of the best in Brazilian popular art. Bulky pieces can be exported.

In the heart of the Ipanema shopping district, two shops specialize in typically Brazilian goods. The Empório Brasil, in a bijou mall at Rua Visconde de Pirajá 595, shop number 108, has a

Left: no shortage of bikinis for sale
Right: straw dolls outside the Cathedral

huge range of tastefully displayed products, from feather and bead art through woodcarving to jewelry. The **Oficina Brasilis**, on the same street, in the basement of another mini-mall at number 580, also offers a fine range of hand-made Brazilian goods.

Open-Air Handicraft Fairs

The **Hippie Market** (Sunday 10am– 6pm)
The **Hippie Market** (Sun 10am– 6pm) is a must if you are in Rio on Sunday (Praça General Osório, eastern end of Ipanema, two blocks from the beach). Makeshift booths offer anything from hand-painted cups to indigenous musical instruments, jewelry, and attractively priced leather goods. The Hippie Fair may have long outlived its name, but it is one of Rio's enduring attractions.

Every evening, from about 7pm in the central reservation of the Copacabana beach road (intersection with Rua Djalma Ulrich), artisans set up stalls and sell their wares – paintings, soccer shirts, hand-made jewelry, and other souvenirs. It's not the Hippie Fair, but if you are not able to be in Rio on a Sunday, it is a reasonable substitute.

Gemstones

Brazil is renowned for its gemstones and creative designers. The mineral reserves ensure a steady supply of world-class gems, and the lively, daring work of many generations of craftsmen ensures that Rio is the place to buy them. The mass market is dominated by two giants, **H. Stern** and **Amsterdam Sauer**, neighbors in Ipanema, at the corner of Rua Visconde de Pirajá and Rua Garcia D'Avila. Both have branches all over the world, and both are owner-operated, and thoroughly reputable. H. Stern opens his workplace to visitors, who, in the course of a 12-minute tour, can watch a raw stone being transformed into a piece of jewelry

(tel: 2259-7442). Even if you buy nothing, visiting these stores is an experience.

Antonio Bernardo is a popular designer, and his funky ideas are popular with the younger crowd. His work can be seen at Rua Garcia D'Avila 121, among other locations, including the São Conrado Fashion Mall. Father-and-son team **Bruno and Flavio Guidi** have been crafting stunning pieces for years. If you are looking for something really special, call them on tel: 2220-7285, or check www.brunoguidi.com.br.

Beachwear

It is no surprise to hear that beachwear is an excellent buy. **Bum Bum** has been dressing women (minimally) for the beach for some 25 years, and is still a strong name. They are at Rua Visconde de Pirajá 351, shop B. Neighboring **Lenny Niemeyer**, in shop 115, is another excellent beachwear designer.

Local Markets

Rio's street markets are an easy way to get to know local produce and see the *cariocas* in action. All manner of fruit and vegetables can be bought in any quantity, so be brave and buy something completely unknown to you. Piles of what look like wilting weeds are actually medicinal herbs, set out on flour sacks. Cookies overflow from bins in station-wagon trunks. The fish trucks all line up together, and nearby you may see someone sitting on a stool filleting freshly bought sardines for shoppers. The display of cut flowers could rival any organized flower show. Vendors start to arrive for the *feira* (market) as early as 4am, and by 3pm there is not a trace of activity left. This is one feature of Rio life that really works, and has not been obliterated by supermarkets.

Some weekday markets in the South Zone are: Monday: Rua Henrique Dumont, Ipanema; Tuesday: Praça General Osório, Ipanema; Wednesday: Rua Maria Eugenia, by the fire station in Humaitá, Botafogo; Thursday: Praça Nossa Senhora Auxiliadora by Flamengo's soccer ground, Leblon; Friday: Praça Nossa Senhora da Paz in Ipanema and Praça Santos Dumont in Gávea (handy for the Botanical Gardens); Saturday: the market in Rua Frei Leandro on the Jardim Botânico side of the Lagoa is chic and fun.

Left: Copacabana handicraft fair

EATING OUT

Brazil's national dish is *feijoada* – black-bean stew. This hearty feast is traditionally consumed at Saturday lunchtime, as it is acknowledged that a rest is needed afterwards. The beans are cooked with salted and dried meats and served with thinly sliced stir-fried kale, and a garnish of sliced oranges and incendiary pepper sauce. Among the city's best *feijoadas* are those served at the premier hotels. Care is taken to separate and label the meats in individual cauldrons, so you know what you are getting.

Brazil's meat is generally excellent and the *churrasco*, or barbecue, is a favorite way of eating it, making *churrascarias (see below)* popular eating places. Fish and seafood are also plentiful and some of the best may be found in the Italian restaurants.

There is a strong Afro-Bahian influence in Brazilian cooking, and spicy fish dishes laced with palm oil, peppers, and coconut make for some memorable meals. *Siri mole*, a soft-shell crab that is a Bahian specialty, should be tried. *Acarajé*, a fritter made of shrimp and beans is another ubiquitous Bahian dish. The traditional accompaniment to many dishes is *farofa*, which looks like sawdust. It is ground manioc, seasoned with garlic and onions, and can be delicious.

You can't beat an ice-cold draft beer – a *chopp* – to chase the heat away. Locally brewed beers are excellent, and light enough to be suited to the climate. The local firewater, *cachaça*, is a sugar-cane spirit, knocked back in shot glasses by the die-hard locals and used to create the *caipirinha*, the nation's drink. Limes are crushed with sugar in the bottom of a glass, which is then filled with ice and *cachaça*. It's heavenly, but it packs a punch. A tamer version uses vodka to make a *caipivodca*.

Brazilian wine is improving all the time, and it is worth asking the wine waiter in smarter restaurants for a local recommendation. Wines produced by Miolo (especially their 'reserva' line), Valduga, and Salton are usually reliable. Chile and Argentina both produce excellent, reasonably priced wines, while European wines tend to be expensive.

Juice bars are everywhere, and the juice is made to order from all manner of exotic fruits – try pineapple and mint, which is extremely refreshing. The bars also serve excellent sandwiches and snacks, which are prepared on the spot so freshness is guaranteed. There is no menu – you can simply point to what you want from the array on glass-enclosed counters. Refreshing *água de côca*, coconut milk drunk with a straw straight from the coconut, is sold in bars and by street vendors.

Eat-all-you-can

Two kinds of restaurant deserve an introduction. The first is the *churrasco rodízio*, or eat-all-you-can barbecue – an experience not to be missed. Large skewers bearing

Above: lunch in the shade at Tia Palmira restaurant

every cut of meat imaginable – such as alligator tails as well as succulent rump steak, chicken, pork, and sausage – are paraded around the restaurant by skillful carvers who lop delicious slices onto the diner's plate. Side dishes of French fries, onion rings, rice, and fried bananas are replenished when only half empty. Colorful buffets of vegetables, salads, and fish dishes offer almost too many choices. Another kind of *rodízio* serves seafood in the same overwhelming quantities and varieties.

'Kilo restaurants' provide an inexpensive way to sample local fare. Pile up your plate with pasta, beans, rice, beef, chicken, and vegetables, which are weighed and charged accordingly. Kilo restaurants are informal and good value, but they fill up in busy areas during the week. Go early, unless you don't mind scraping the bottom of the pan.

Restaurants are obliged to affix their menus by the front door, and are also obliged to set aside an area for non-smokers, although at peak times this requirement can be hard to fulfill. Usually, you will be presented with an array of breads, olives, and patés when you sit down; this is optional and it is not free, so you can refuse it.

The following listing is selective. There are hundreds of restaurants in the cheap and cheerful category, and you can tell at a glance if they are appropriate to your mood and fancy. We have singled out restaurants we think are special in one way or another, or

that you might not otherwise come across. They are located in areas in which you are likely to find yourself. They accept most major credit cards, but phone ahead to ensure that your card is acceptable. In many restaurants, portions are huge, and sharing a dish *(para dividir)* is standard practice.

Price guide:
Approximate prices are based on a two-course meal for two. Wine is not included, but a decent bottle should cost about U$15–20; cheaper wines are available, and you can, of course, spend much more.

$	under US$25
$$	US$25–80
$$$	over US$80

Top Choices
Cipriani
Copacabana Palace Hotel
Avenida Atlântica 1703, Copacabana
Tel: 2555-7070
Daily 12.30–3pm, 7pm–1am.
For very special occasions, sumptuous décor, imaginative menu. The sister restaurant to Venice's Cipriani, and voted one of the 10 best hotel restaurants in the world.
$$$

Garcia & Rodrigues
Avenida Ataulfo de Paiva 1251, Leblon
Tel: 2512-8188
Daily 8am–midnight.
Freshly baked bread and pastries, snacks,

Above: a selection of local specialties

as well as a gourmet's dream of an *à la carte* menu and wine list. $–$$$

Uniquely Brazilian

Academia da Cachaça
Rua Conde de Bernadote 26, Leblon
Tel: 2239-1542
Daily noon–1am. No credit cards.
This fun, informal bar is the headquarters for connoisseurs of *cachaça*. Try some of the mysteries on the snack menu for an authentically local taste. Either side of the Academia are other bars and restaurants. $

Azul Marinho
Rua Francisco Otaviano 177, Ipanema
Hotel Arpoador Inn
Tel: 2513-5014
Daily noon–midnight.
A sea view at the end of Ipanema beach is the backdrop for some fine Brazilian seafood. Reservations are recommended. $$

Casa da Feijoada
Rua Prudente de Morais 10, Ipanema
Tel: 2523-4994/2247-2776
Daily noon–midnight.
Although *feijoada* is usually reserved for Saturday, you can sample it all through the week at this Ipanema location. $$

Marius Crustáceos
Avenida Atlântica 290A, Copacabana
Tel: 2543-6363
Mon–Fri noon–4pm, 6pm–midnight, Sat–Sun noon–last customer.
Just about every kind of marine creature is served on the all-you-can-eat system. Pricey, but worth it. $$$

Porção
Rua Barão da Torre 218, Ipanema
Tel: 2522-0999
Avenida Armando Lombardi 591, Barra
Tel: 2493-3355
Porção Rio's (view of Guanabara Bay)
Aterro do Flamengo, no number
Tel: 2554-8535/2554-7337
Daily 11am–1am.
All three branches are a carnivore's paradise, but with plenty of veggie and fishy options. Graze at the buffet, then meat is carved onto your plate. Not cheap, but must be tried. $$$

Siri Mole
Rua Francisco Otaviano 50, Ipanema
Tel: 2267-0894/2523-4240
Mon 7pm–last customer; Tues–Sun noon–last customer.
An excellent exponent of the Afro-Brazilian style of cooking – fish stews redolent of palm oil and peppers – conveniently located where Ipanema joins Copacabana. $$$

Yemanjá
Rua Visconde de Pirajá 128A, Ipanema
Tel: 2247-7004
Daily noon–midnight.
Specializing in the cuisine of Bahia – plenty of peppers and aromatic fish stews. Handy for the Sunday Hippie Fair. $$

International

Boteco 66 (pronounced *boteko meia meia*)
Rua Alexandre Ferreira 66, Lagoa/Jardim Botânico
Tel: 2266-0838
Daily noon–last customer.
A large, weather-proofed veranda filled with pretty oddments sets the scene for memorable meals, chosen from a limited but excellent French-inspired menu. Also handy for the Botanical Gardens. $$

Don Camillo
Avenida Atlântica 3056, Copacabana
Tel: 2549-9958
Daily noon–midnight.
Try for a table on the sidewalk as the indoor area can be rowdy. The wandering minstrels haven't far to wander so they can be a bit deafening. Italian food, fish a specialty. $$

Madame Butterfly
Rua Barão da Torre 472, Ipanema
Tel: 2267-4347
Daily noon–2am.
Combines sophistication with an innovative approach to Japanese cuisine. $$

Osteria D'Angollo
Rua Paul Redfern 40, Ipanema
Tel: 2259-3148
Daily noon–4pm, 6pm–midnight.
Carefully prepared and tasty Italian food served in

Right: oysters fresh from the sea to the table

stylish surroundings. Risottos a specialty. Other options beckon nearby on 'Restaurant Corner.' $$$

Satyricon
Rua Barão da Torre 192, Ipanema
Tel: 2521-0627
Tues–Sat noon–2am, Sun noon–midnight, Mon 6pm–midnight.
An Italian take on cooking fish to perfection, with star-gazing thrown in. $$$

Sushi Leblon
Rua Dias Ferreira 256, Leblon
Tel: 2274-1342
Mon–Fri 7pm–1.30am, Sat 1–4.30pm, 7pm–1.30am, Sun 1.30pm–midnight.
Serves trendy, top-quality Japanese food that attracts the beautiful people. $$

Typically Rio
Allegro Bistrô
Modern Sound Mega Music Store
Rua Barata Ribeiro 502D, Copacabana
Tel: 2548-5005
Mon–Sat 9am–8pm.
Rio's finest music store provides an unusual backdrop for a snack or a light meal. $

Club Chocolate
São Conrado Fashion Mall
Estrada da Gávea 899, São Conrado
Tel: 3322-1223
Noon–midnight.
Hidden behind a chic dress shop. Innovative combinations, with an Italian slant, this is designer food at its best. $$$

Confeitaria Colombo
Rua Gonçalves Dias 32, Centro
Tel: 2232-2300
Mon–Fri 8am–8pm, Sat 9.30am–5pm.
Forte de Copacabana
Avenida Atlântica
Tues–Sun 10am–8pm.
A 100-year-old Rio tradition. The downtown location is sumptuously *belle époque*. The café in the fortress serves simple meals in a stunning setting, with great views. $$

Esplanada Grill
Rua Barão da Torre 600, Ipanema
Tel: 2512-2970

Mon–Fri noon–4pm, 7pm–midnight, Sat–Sun noon–midnight.
A great place to see and be seen, with a wide-ranging menu, strong on meat. You might just get the perfect steak here. $$$

Garota da Urca
Avenida João Luis Alves 56, Urca
Tel: 2541-8585
Noon–midnight.
Simple fare in a spectacular setting, at the base of Sugar Loaf mountain. $

Gula Gula
Rua Rita Ludolf 87, Leblon
Tel: 2294-8792
Rua Aníbal de Mendonça 132, Ipanema
Tel: 2259-3084
Daily noon–midnight.
Rua Primeiro de Março 23, Centro
Tel: 3852-1174
Mon–Fri lunchtime.
Oodles of well-prepared choices in these comfortable and efficient eateries. $$

La Mole
Rua Dias Ferreira 147, Leblon
Tel: 2294-0699
Avenida Nossa Senhora de Copacabana 552, Copacabana
Tel: 2235-3366
Av. Lauro Muller 116, shop 101, Botafogo
Inside Rio Sul Shopping Center
Tel: 2542-4641
Daily 11am–1pm.
Old-fashioned Italian fare as well as steaks and other options. The initial snacks are generous, so you may not need a first course. Popular, and busy on weekends. $$

Above: the snack bar at Corcovado
Right: when the sun goes down, Rio lights up

NIGHTLIFE

Cariocas have boundless energy. Although they don't indulge in an afternoon siesta, they seem to be able to party all night, every night. Every season sees a new bar take over the scene, so make inquiries as to what's 'in' while you are here. The weekly news magazine *Veja*, published on Sunday, contains a glossy insert called *Vejinha*, packed with listings of events. Rio is one of the world's major gay-friendly destinations, and the initials 'GLS' in a listing indicates that the event caters to the gay community.

As ever, let caution be your companion when out on the town. International rules apply: don't accept drinks from strangers; find out beforehand how much and what you are paying for. And at the slightest sign of a scuffle, hit the road.

A Night at the Races

Nestling between the Lagoa and the Botanical Gardens, the **Jockey Club** (tel: 2512-9988) is serious business. Visitors are welcome to spend an evening in the members' stand; there is no charge and no identification is needed, because what the Jockey Club wants is to get visitors in there and laying bets. There are several bars and restaurants on site, so you can make an evening of it. On Monday, the first race is at 6pm, on Friday at 4pm, at weekends, the first race is at 2pm, the last at 7pm. Visitors wearing sandals or beachwear will not be admitted but the overall tone in this Louis XV-style palace is extremely casual. The Jockey Club has several clubhouses around Rio, so make sure you tell the cab driver you want Jockey Clube na Praça Santos Dumont, Gávea.

Classical Music

It is worth checking the local press if you are interested in classical music. At any time of the year you may be able to attend a world-class concert in the sumptuous setting of the **Theatro Municipal**, Praça Floriano (tel: 2277-4141) or the more modern **Sala Cecília Meirelles**, Largo da Lapa (tel: 2224-3913), both in downtown Rio, at a fraction of what it would cost you back home. www.viva-musica.com.br is a useful site for finding out in advance what's on.

Samba School Rehearsals

Samba, which is now the national music of Brazil, evolved in the 19th century as the music of the poor, predominantly black, sections of society. It became mainstream and popular in the 1930s and was recognized as an important element in Carnival some 20 years later. At most times of the year, a fun but somewhat challenging way to experience samba is by attending one of the rehearsals for the Carnival parade held by the major

samba schools. A point to bear in mind is that the schools only sing one song all the way through the parade, so that may be the only song you will hear. Rehearsals are usually held in out-of-the way places that you would not normally visit, so caution is especially necessary for this exciting evening. The local press carries dates and venues of rehearsals; do ask for help from your hotel in planning this outing.

Samba Shows

The **Churrascaria Plataforma**, Rua Adalberto Ferreira 32, Leblon (tel: 2274-4022) is home to one of Rio's traditions, the samba show, performed nightly in the upstairs theater. Downstairs is the *churrascaria*, offering a varied menu as well as huge portions of beef. Adjacent is the 350-seat **Bar do Tom**, named in honor of its late, great patron, Antonio (Tom) Carlos Jobim. While it may not be the most adventurous way to see the gorgeous ladies in feathers, it is safe, well-organized and punctual. The show starts at 10pm and lasts approximately one and a half hours; the cost is about U\$35.

Live Music Bars

A number of bars stage pocket shows all year round. Always phone ahead to ensure there will be live music. At many places, you pay a small entrance fee, called the *couvert artístico*, which generally goes to pay the musicians. If you are asked to pay *consumação mínima*, this means you have to spend a stipulated, but usually very reasonable, amount on food and drink. These establishments pride themselves on the quality of their music, and make room on the agenda for fledgling groups in addition to well-known bands. The three places listed below are in the bohemian centre of Rio, the district called Lapa. Keep your wits about you, and do not stray too far away from the recommended sites.

Rio Scenarium
Rua do Lavradio 20, Lapa
Tel: 2233-3239, 3852-5516
Part antique shop, part bar, part restaurant, part dance hall. Excellent music. Tues 8pm, Wed–Fri 6.30pm, Sat 7.30pm.

Casa da Mãe Joana
Avenida Gomes Freire 547, Lapa
Tel: 2224-4071
Plenty of dancing and reasonably priced snacks at this popular haunt. Live music Thur 8pm, Fri–Sat 7pm.

Carioca da Gema
Rua Mem de Sá 79, Lapa
Tel: 2221-0043
Each night of the week (Mon–Sat) is devoted to a different style of music in the rich Brazilian repertoire. Mon–Thur 9pm, Fri 8.30pm, Sat 9pm.

Open-Air Attractions

Dotted around Lagoa Rodrigo de Freitas are numerous kiosks, where you can sit at a table and soak up the views. Some are themed – Arab or German for example – others have live performances. On a fine night, these spots offer a memorable, relaxing evening.

Other open-air options can be found at two unlikely locations – farmers' markets in Leblon and Botafogo. **Cobal Leblon** is handily located near the Plataforma and by day functions as a produce market. In the evening tables are set out and the beer flows. The **Botafogo Cobal** is in an area that has little else to attract visitors, but is great fun and worth a visit. Both are inexpensive.

Bars
Botequim Informal
This popular chain of noisy, busy bars are full of character and fun.

Left: close up in Botafogo

Rua Humberto de Campos 646, Leblon
Tel: 2259-6967
Av. das Américas, 500, Barra da Tijuca
Tel: 2492-2995
Rua Conde de Bernadote, 26, Leblon
Tel: 2540-7561
R. Barão da Torre, 348, Ipanema

Casa da Matriz
Rua Henrique de Novaes 107, Botafogo
Tel: 2266-1014
Multi-purpose, late-night destination with loud music on two dance floors. Open till the wee hours.

Esch Café
Rua Dias Ferreira 78, Leblon
Tel: 2512-5651
Cigar-smokers' heaven, serving fanciful cocktails and occasional live music. There are other excellent options in the same street.

Garota de Ipanema
Rua Vinícius de Morais 49A, Ipanema
Tel: 2523-3787
Where the famous *Girl from Ipanema* was written, scribbled on the back of a napkin. Great beer, tasty snacks, unbeatable people-watching, and it's inexpensive.

Melt
Rua Rita Ludolf 47, Leblon
Tel: 2249-9309
Every night is different as a variety of DJs

impose their styles on the dance floor. Don't bother getting there before 10pm.

Mistura Fina
Avenida Borges de Medeiros 3207, Lagoa/ Jardim Botânico
Tel: 2537-2844
As its name suggests, this is a fine mixture of bar, restaurant, and venue for some excellent music. Reservations are recommended.

The Lord Jim Pub
Rua Paul Redfern 32, Ipanema
Tel: 2259-3047
The name says it all. A great place to pick up tips from foreign residents and visitors.

OO
Rua Padre Leonel Franca 240, Gávea
Tel: 2540-8041
Lively, well-appointed dance spot in Rio's Planetarium. Music runs the gamut from funk through samba and jazz.

Sindicato do Chopp
Avenida Atlântica 514, Leme
Tel: 2541-3133
The Beerdrinker's Union, noisy, fun and full of laughter. Great location on Leme beach.

A word of warning: the **Help** disco on Copacabana beachfront is notorious. It has been said that if you go to Help, you may end up needing it.

Above: a quiet moment in a *favela* bar

CALENDAR OF EVENTS

Festivals are not a notable feature of Rio life in the way they are in most other South American countries, but local holidays are taken very seriously indeed. Schools and banks close and beaches and highways fill up. The day of the week on which these holidays occur is important. A Monday or Friday holiday automatically provides a long weekend; holidays that fall on Tuesday and Thursday also tend to lead to even longer weekends, but the intervening days are not official holidays, and schools, banks, and shops will open. They are, however, treated as holidays and are occasions when thousands of people either leave the city or enter it, causing massive traffic jams, especially in the summer months.

When booking your holiday, or when you are planning an out-of-town trip, it makes sense to check these dates to avoid any nasty surprises.

Carnival

You either come to Rio, or you come to Rio's Carnival. The city becomes a different place during the magical week, and all routines are disrupted. Bus timetables change; museums and other attractions close down. Bars and restaurants are either packed with revelers or close down for the entire period, if the owners fear damage and mayhem. Entire streets, and even neighborhoods, are closed

to traffic of all kinds, except for people wearing a silly costume or a bathing suit.

Carnival usually takes place in February, but exact dates vary as it is a pre-Lent festival and therefore linked to the date of Easter. The keys to the city of Rio are ceremoniously handed over to the King of Carnival on the Friday afternoon preceding Shrove Tuesday. Officially, normality returns on Ash Wednesday, but in practice this is increasingly a whole week of holiday, when many *cariocas* flee the city to outlying resorts and many others stay and dance till they drop.

The weeks leading up to Carnival provide some extra attractions for visitors, in the form of major samba school rehearsals *(see pages 75–6)*. Check the local press for times and locations.

Easter

Easter Monday is not a holiday in Brazil, but Good Friday is. The week leading up to Easter Sunday is *Semana Santa*, Holy Week, and is observed by the majority of practicing Catholics in the city. It also, naturally, involves a long weekend.

Corpus Christi

The moveable feast of Corpus Christi always produces a potential long weekend, as it falls on the second Thursday after Pentecost (the date depends on Easter, but it is usually in mid-June).

Above: New Year is celebrated with extravagant firework displays

All Souls' Day

All Souls' Day on November 2 is an important day when the dead are revered and visited. The price of flowers shoots up as millions of *cariocas* lay tributes at cemeteries all over the city, causing havoc to traffic. Masses are said hourly at all principal burial grounds. It is not only family members who receive a visit on this day of collective mourning. Stars of screen, radio, and sport also get a visit from their loyal fans.

Christmas

Brazilians celebrate Christmas with a late-night feast on Christmas Eve, leaving Christmas day free for recovering from the feasting and possibly going to the beach.

New Year's Eve

New Year's Eve has become a major event in Rio. 'The largest public party in the world' ranges almost city-wide, but Copacabana is where the majority of foreign visitors will join the other 2 million revelers. The countdown starts weeks before the magic moment of midnight. Throughout December, weather permitting, shows are held at temporary amphitheaters on the beach, where the best in Brazilian musical talent can be enjoyed.

Traffic into Copacabana is restricted to buses and cabs, and the drum beats become louder as the sun goes down. Entrepreneurs set up wobbly portable barbecues and provide tasty morsels to keep you going. At the other end of the spectrum, the city's premier hotels put on reservations-only banquets with live bands and every amenity.

But while it is party time for most people it is a solemn day of veneration for the followers of *macumba*, the local religion that mixes elements of Catholicism with others of African origin. New Year is sacred to Yemanjá, a vain goddess to whom offerings of scent and toiletries are sent out to sea in little boats, festooned with white gladioli.

The following are the main holidays and festivals in Rio *(also see page 85)*:

January

1   New Year's Day
20 São Sebastián: Saint Sebastian's Day (patron saint of Rio)

Right: Carnival samba parade

February/March

Carnival Sunday dates, 2006–10
2006   27 February
2007   18 February
2008   3 February
2009   22 February
2010   14 February

April

21 Tiradentes Day
23 St George's Day

May

1   Labor Day

June

Corpus Christi (dates vary)

September

7   Declaration of Independence Day

October

12 Nossa Senhora de Aparecida (patron saint of Brazil)
    Commerce Day (shops closed; dates vary)

November

2   All Souls' Day
15 Proclamation of the Republic
20 Black Conscience Day

December

24 Christmas Eve
25 Christmas Day
31 New Year's Eve and feast of the goddess Yemanjá

Practical Information

GETTING THERE

By Air

Rio is served by two airports, the Rio de Janeiro-Galeão (Antonio Carlos Jobim) International Airport, on Ilha do Governador about 20km (13 miles) north of the city; and the domestic Santos Dumont Airport in downtown Rio. Numerous airlines fly to Rio, but most of them do so via São Paulo, which can add an irritating couple of hours to the journey. Try for a direct flight if possible. If you plan to visit other cities in Brazil, check out the Brazil Airpass at your point of origin; this can significantly reduce the cost of otherwise expensive internal flights within Brazil.

To get out of the airport and into Rio, the preferred form of transport is a taxi. You buy your fixed-price ticket within the terminal building itself, and so are safe from any unscrupulous drivers lurking outside the building (as an example, the fare from the international airport to Copacabana is approximately US$25).

Inexpensive, air-conditioned buses leave the airport at half-hourly intervals, starting at 5.30am; the last one leaves the airport at 11.10pm. The final destination of the bus is the Alvorada Terminal in Barra. Santos Dumont Airport in downtown Rio is the first stop. From there, the bus follows the coast along Flamengo, Botafogo, Copacabana, Ipanema, Leblon, Vidigal, São Conrado and on to Barra. This route is altered during the morning rush hour, 7–10am, when all lanes along the coast road lead into the city. The bus is then obliged to take the next road inland from its usual route. From the Alvorada Terminal in Barra, for the return journey, the first bus also leaves at 5.30am, the last at 11.10pm. Passengers must flag this bus down, as there are no official stops.

Duty Free: Remember that you can use the well-stocked duty free shop at the airport on arrival, as well as departure. You cannot pay with reais, however; use any other currency, or an international credit card. US dollars are the easiest for change.

Airport Tax: The airport tax at Rio International Airport is considered high at approximately US$36, so make sure that you keep back enough cash (in reais or US dollars) to pay this on your way out. To find out the exact value at the time you travel, call the information section of the airport, tel: 2298-4525/4526.

By Sea

There are no regular passenger lines serving Rio, but it is very much on the cruise lines' itineraries, especially over New Year's Eve and Carnival.

TRAVEL ESSENTIALS

When to Visit

Despite the often oppressive heat and soaring humidity, Rio receives its greatest number of visitors during the period from December to March, when the city's premier parties, New Year's Eve and Carnival, both take place. Hotel prices soar at this time of the year. The mid-year break for local school children is the month of July, which

Left: boarding the Corcovado train
Right: Santa Teresa street signs

is when many residents take their holidays. Temperatures in the middle of the year are more amenable and it rains less.

Visas and Passports

In these days of heightened international security, it makes sense to check your particular status in terms of the need for a visa to enter Brazil. Generally speaking, passports must be valid for six months from the date of arrival in Brazil, and you may be asked to present your return ticket. When you get your passport stamped, retain your half of the immigration form, as you will need to surrender it when you leave the country. Visitors are admitted for an initial 90-day period, which may be extended at the discretion of the Federal Police.

Vaccinations

If you have traveled to any of the following countries in the three months preceding your arrival in Brazil, you will need to produce proof of inoculation against yellow fever: Angola, Benin, Bolivia, Burkina Faso, Cameroon, Colombia, Democratic Republic of Congo, Ecuador, French Guyana, Gabon, Gambia, Ghana, Guinea Bissau, Liberia, Nigeria, Peru, Sierra Leone, Sudan, Venezuela, and Zaire. If you plan to visit other areas of Brazil, especially the jungles, plan for a yellow-fever vaccination at least 10 days before arrival. Otherwise, no vaccinations are required for Rio de Janeiro.

Customs

Customs formalities can be slow at Rio airport, so keep your sense of humor about you. Most visitors sail through the baggage checks with no problems, but be prepared to take your chances on the supposedly random selection of baggage to be inspected. You hit a button on a pillar: if you get a green light you carry on through, while a red light means you open your baggage to inspection. Fresh food, plants, and seeds may be confiscated, and be prepared for strife if you are carrying what might be considered commercial quantities of anything. Entering Brazil with illegal drugs is an immediate invitation to disaster.

Weather

Summer officially runs from December through March, with temperatures rarely below the 29°C (84°F) mark and soaring to boiling point; it is also a time of heavy rainfall and high humidity. Autumn – April to June – is a fine time to visit Rio, with temperatures in the 18°–30°C (64°–86°F) range. Winter temperatures hover between 14–23°C (57–73°F). Spring, which can be wet, runs from September to December, when thermometers show 18°–27°C (64°–80°F).

Clothing

Brazilians rarely dress formally, but usually manage to look smart. Shorts and bermudas are fine most of the time, but not in the down-

Above: the dominant faith is Roman Catholicism

town area, nor when visiting some historic sites, such as churches. Air-conditioning can produce arctic conditions in restaurants and on long-haul bus journeys, so a long-sleeved top or light jacket may be needed.

Electricity
While most of the better hotels will provide a 220-volt outlet, the standard for Rio is 110 volts, 60 cycles.

Time Differences
Rio is 3 hours behind GMT and 2 hours ahead of EST.

GETTING ACQUAINTED

Geography
Squeezed between mountains and the sea, Rio lies just north of the Tropic of Capricorn, at latitude 22.5°. Misleadingly, the western part of the city, comprising Leblon, Ipanema, and Copacabana, most frequented by visitors, is known as the South Zone (Zona Sul), while the eastern part of the city, where the airport is located, is known as the North Zone (Zona Norte). Rio is not a difficult place in which to keep your bearings, as the beach and other landmarks such as the Sugar Loaf and Corcovado mountains are constant points of reference. The major attractions are relatively well-signposted; other parts of the city are not.

Government and Economy
Brazil is a democracy led by a president elected by direct vote. If the 1980s saw chaos

in varying degrees in both government and the economy, the 1990s consolidated Brazil's viability on the world economic scene. Enormous natural wealth, seemingly endless fertile land, and relatively cheap labor make Brazil a significant player on the international scene. Social inequality, however, persists, and the gap between the rich and the poor is still vast.

Religion
Religious tolerance is widely practiced in Brazil. The dominant faith is Roman Catholicism, sometimes combined with one of the Afro-Brazilian cults. Evangelical congregations are a relatively new but immensely powerful element in Brazilian society.

Population
The population of Greater Rio de Janeiro is approximately 6 million. The largest contingent of immigrants is the Portuguese colony but, as one would expect from a city as cosmopolitan as Rio, numerous nationalities are present. Due to the difficulties of living off the land in Brazil's interior, all the major cities receive droves of immigrants from the poorer rural states, in an often-futile search for an easier life.

MONEY MATTERS

Currency
The legal tender in Brazil is the real (plural reais), sub-divided into 100 centavos. Paper money comes in the following denominations of reais: 100, 50, 20, 10, 5, 2, and 1. Coins are 1, 5, 10, 25, and 50 centavos and 1 real. Coins have never been taken very seriously here. While lack of change is not a big problem, don't try to pay for a 10 real taxi ride with a 100 real bill.

Foreign currency is not generally accepted; personal checks drawn on an overseas bank are definitely not accepted.

Exchange
Look for signs for *Câmbio*. US dollars are by far the easiest currency to exchange into reais. Banks and exchange bureaux charge a commission on transactions, and are required to display publicly the net rate for the day. You get a better rate for cash than for travelers'

Left: the boys just want to have fun

cheques. The exchange bureau at Rio's international airport functions from 8am–10pm daily. With the stabilization of the Brazilian currency, black-market transactions have ceased to be a feature of life.

Exchange rates (2005) are approximately US$1 = 2.6 reais, £1 = 5 reais.

Credit Cards

Credit cards are widely used, but always check the acceptability of your particular card before making a purchase. Visa and MasterCard are the cards best represented.

Cash Machines

Technically, you should have no trouble getting cash out of an ATM with your card. For your own peace of mind, however, it makes sense to check this before you run out of cash. If you encounter difficulties, try going to a branch of the Banco do Brasil or Citibank, remembering to take your sense of humor with you.

Taxes

All prices shown are net, i.e. they show what you actually have to pay, as the tax is built into the price.

Tipping

A 10 or even 15 percent service charge is usually added to restaurant bills, but even so, an additional tip is often given. If you are paying with a credit card, a tip in cash will be especially welcome as it will be available immediately, instead of when the card transaction is cleared. Taxi drivers also appreciate a tip, even of the small, rounding-up variety.

GETTING AROUND

Taxis

Taxis are the standard form of transport for visitors (and, indeed, many residents) in Rio. Regular taxis are yellow, with a blue stripe down the side. They are metered, and there is a 'getting-in' charge, which is shown on the meter when you board. After 9pm and on weekends, a surcharge comes into effect, and the number 2 will be displayed on the meter. As an example, for your guidance, the standard daytime fare from Copacabana to the Botanical Gardens should be approximately US$4. Taxi drivers are *not* allowed to charge extra for turning on the air-conditioning, even if they try to convince you that they are.

Rio's radio taxis are more expensive than the regular yellow cabs, but extremely professional and reliable. If you wish to pay by credit card, advise them when you make your reservation. Reliable service is provided by JB Radio Taxi, tel: 2501-3026; Central de Taxi, tel: 2593-2598; Coopsind, tel: 2589-4503; Coopertramo Radiotaxi, tel: 2560-2022; and Transcoopas, tel: 2590-6891.

Be wary of using car services stationed outside the five-star hotels, as they charge what they will.

Train/Metro

Rio's conventional rail network serves the suburbs and is of little use to the foreign visitor. The Metro, on the other hand, is clean, well-organized, and efficient. It operates Monday–Saturday 5am–midnight, Sunday 7am–11pm. Information available on tel: 0800-595-1111 (Mon–Sat 8am–8pm).

Line 1 links Copacabana (Estação Siqueira Campos) to Praça Saens Peña in Tijuca. This line is the most useful for visitors as it calls at Botafogo, Flamengo, Largo do Machado, Catete, Glória, Cinelândia, Carioca, Uruguaiana, and Presidente Vargas. Line 2 is of less interest, as it serves the suburbs, which have little to offer the visitor.

Bus

Rio's regular city buses have a reputation all of their own, and caution should be exercised at all times when using them.

Long-haul buses, however, are efficient, safe, and reliable. Call the Rodoviária Novo Rio, tel: 3213-1800 for general information. Búzios is served by the 1001 bus company, tel: 2625-1001 or 2625-0577. The Costa Verde bus company, tel: 2233-3809, connects Rio to the western coast, Angra dos Reis, and Paraty. Petrópolis is served by two companies, Fácil and Única, which are both on tel: 2263-8792.

Car

Driving in Rio can be quite a challenge, especially in the rain and during rush hours. The major car-rental companies have offices in Rio, and it is also possible to hire a car and driver for the day. Due to the difficulty of parking in Rio itself, visitors are advised to consider renting a car only for visits to outlying beaches or for the excursions to Búzios and Paraty.

Hertz has offices in Copacabana at Avenida Princesa Isabel, tel: 2275-7440; at the GaleãoInternational Airport, tel: 3398-4338; and at Santos Dumont Airport, tel: 2262-0612.

Avis operates out of Avenida Princesa Isabel in Copacabana, tel: 2543-8481; the GaleãoInternational Airport, tel: 3398-5060; and Santos Dumont Airport, tel: 3814-7378.

HOURS AND HOLIDAYS

Business Hours

Offices generally function Monday–Friday 8am–6pm. Banking hours are 10am–4pm, but exchange transactions only take place during part of the working day. The large shopping malls are generally open Monday–Saturday 10am–10pm, Sunday 3–9pm (see *Shopping, page 69* for details on individual malls).

Public Holidays

January 1 New Year's Day
January20 São Sebastián: Saint Sebastian's Day (Rio only)
February/March Carnival (dates vary – *see Calendar of Events, page 78*)
March/April Good Friday (dates vary)
April 21 Tiradentes Day
April 23 St George's Day
May 1 Labor Day
June Corpus Christi (dates vary)
September 7 Declaration of Independence Day
October 12 Nossa Senhora de Aparecida (patron saint of Brazil)
October Commerce Day (shops closed; dates vary)
November 2 All Souls' Day
November 15 Proclamation of the Republic
November 20 Black Conscience Day
December 24 Christmas Eve
December 25 Christmas Day
December 31 New Year's Eve and feast of Yemanjá (half-day holiday)

ACCOMMODATIONS

Hotels

Proximity to the beach is a key pricing factor, and good deals can be had at hotels that are not actually on, but are within walking distance of, the beach. Check when booking whether breakfast is included. Add 10 percent service plus 5 percent tax to the rates you are quoted. Some hotels offer free transport to and from the airport. All the hotels listed have swimming pools, unless otherwise noted.

A newcomer to the hotel scene is 'Cama e Café' – Bed and Breakfast – a network of private homes in the bohemian Santa Teresa area. Properties range from 1900s mansions to picturesque artists' workshops; prices are appropriate to the degree of comfort offered. There is no minimum-stay period. Find out more from www.camaecafe.com.br.

Motels in Brazil charge by the hour: they are for lovers, not tourists.

All hotel rates vary seasonally, and rocket during New Year and Carnival. The rates

Left: the tram is not the fastest form of transport but it may be the most fun

indicated below are for a standard double room with bath.

Price Guide

$$$$	over U$300
$$$	US$200–300
$$	US$100–200
$	under US$100

(Hotels are listed alphabetically within their price categories.)

Copacabana

Copacabana Palace Hotel
Avenida Atlântica 1702
Tel: 2548-7070
Fax: 2235-7330
www.copacabanapalace.orient-express.com
Beachfront location. The lap of luxury, with gracious hospitality at its international best, in the beautifully refurbished 'Palace by the Sands.' $$$$

Rio Othon Palace
Avenida Atlântica 3264
Tel: 2522-1522
Fax: 2521-1697
www.hoteis-othon.com.br
Beachfront. The Othon Group offers a wide range of hotels in Rio de Janeiro and other Brazilian cities. Top of the line is the huge Othon Palace, right in the thick of things on Copacabana beach. $$$$

J. W. Marriott Hotel
Avenida Atlântica 2600
Tel: 2545-6500
Fax: 2545-6555
www.marriott.com
Beachfront. All you would expect from a top-of-the-line hotel – luxury, technology, and service. Rooftop fitness center. $$$

Augusto's Copacabana
Rua Bolivar 119
Tel: 2547-1800
Fax: 2549-6118
www.augustoshotel.com.br
Two blocks from the beach. Well appointed; sauna and Jacuzzi. $$

Excelsior Copacabana Hotel
Avenida Atlântica 1800
Tel: 2545-6000

Fax: 2257-1850
www.windsorhoteis.com
Beachfront. Part of the Windsor Group, which operates a small chain of hotels with a good reputation for their friendly and attentive service. Well located. $$

Le Meridien Copacabana
Avenida Altântica 1020, Leme
Tel: 3873-8888
Fax: 3873-8777
www.lemeridien-copacabana.com
Full service to international standard. Good access to excellent Leme beach and restaurants, at northeast end of Copacabana; handy for Rio Sul shopping center. $$

Luxor Regente
Avenida Atlântica 3716
Tel: 2525-2070
Fax: 2267-7693
www.luxor-hoteis.com.br
Beachfront. The Luxor Group has three hotels in Copacabana and has always offered reasonable value. This one has a gym and business center. The other two are the **Luxor Copacabana**, also beachfront, and the **Luxor Continental**, one block from Leme beach. All in same price bracket. $$

Miramar Palace Hotel
Avenida Atlântica 3668
Tel: 2525-0303
Fax: 2521-3294
www.windsorhoteis.com
Beachfront. Another member of the Windsor Group. Spacious rooms; gym and sauna, and lovely rooftop bar. $$

Plaza Copacabana
Avenida Princesa Isabel 263
Tel: 2275-07722
Fax: 2257-1850
www.windsorhoteis.com
Well located on the avenue that separates Copacabana from Leme. $$

Rio Internacional Hotel
Avenida Atlantica 1500
Tel: 2546-8000
Fax: 2542-5443
www.riointernacional.com.br
Beachfront. Modern, functional, and

friendly; well suited to both the business and leisure traveler; just 10 minutes by taxi from downtown Rio. $$

Windsor Palace
Rua Domingos Ferreira 7
Tel: 2545-9000
Fax: 2549-9373
www.windsorhoteis.com.br
Only a short walk away from the beach. Another hotel in the well-regarded Windsor Group chain, and as friendly and attentive as the rest. $$

Benidorm Palace Hotel
Rua Barata Ribeiro 547
Tel: 2548-8880
Fax: 2256-6369
Two blocks from Copacabana beach, the Benidorm offers value for money in an action-packed location. $

Grandarrel Ouro Verde Hotel
Avenida Atlântica 1456
Tel: 2543-4123
Fax: 2543-4776
www.grandarrell.com
Beachfront; Art Deco style hotel. Roomy. The rates for the back-facing rooms make it a good deal. $–$$

Majestic Rio Palace
Rua Cinco de Julho 195
Tel: 2548-2030
Fax: 2255-1692

www.majestichotel.com.br
Set back from Copacabana beach, this is a modern hotel well-known for its friendly service. $

Ipanema
Caesar Park
Avenida Vieira Souto 460
Tel: 2525-2525
Fax: 2521-6000
www.caesar-park.com.br
Beachfront. Located at one of the hot spots of Ipanema beach, this is a modern member of the Leading Hotels of the World Group. $$$

Arpoador Inn
Rua Francisco Otaviano 177
Tel: 2523-0060
Fax. 2511-0194
Well located at the Copacabana end of Ipanema beach. Rooms without a sea view are a bargain; those with a sea view are still fairly reasonable. $$

Everest Rio
Avenida Prudente de Morais 1117
Tel: 2525-2200
Fax: 2521-3198
www.everest.com.br
One block from the beach. Conveniently located in the heart of Ipanema, just a stone's throw from the beach and serious shopping, the Everest has long been a favorite place for families. $$

Above: Ipanema promenade

Ipanema Plaza
Rua Farme de Amoedo 34
Tel: 3687-2000/3687-2121
Fax: 3687-2001
www.ipanemaplaza.com.br
Excellent location in Ipanema, an easy walk from the beach. $$

Mar Ipanema
Rua Visconde de Pirajá 539
Tel: 2512-9898
Fax: 2511-4038
www.maripanema.com
Modern, in the heart of Ipanema shopping country, just two blocks from the beach. $$

Sol Ipanema
Avenida Vieira Souto 320
Tel: 2525-2020
Fax: 2247-8484
www.solipanema.com.br
Beachfront. A member of the Best Western Group, the Sol Ipanema has great views and friendly service. $$

Everest Park
Rua Maria Quitéria 19
Tel: 2525-2200
Fax: 2521-3198
www.everest.com.br
Small hotel just around the corner from the Everest Rio *(see above)*; guests may use the larger hotel's facilities. $

Leblon
Marina Palace
Avenida Delfim Moreira 630, Leblon
Tel: 2172-1000
Fax: 2172-1010
www.hotelmarina.com.br
Beachfront. The Marina Palace is full of charm and well appointed. A little further up Leblon beach is the **Marina All Suites**, which is also delightful (the latter is in the $$$ price range). $$

Leblon Palace Hotel
Avenida Ataulfo de Paiva 204, Leblon
Tel: 2512-8000
Fax: 2274-5741
www.leblonpalace.com.br
Very well located in Leblon 'village', on the border of Ipanema. $

Barra da Tijuca
Sheraton Barra Hotel and Suites
Avenida Lúcio Costa 3150
Tel: 3139-8000
Fax: 3139-8085
www.sheraton-rio.com
Beachfront. All you would expect from an international resort hotel, and half an hour by taxi from Ipanema. $$

Ocean Drive
Avenida Sernambetiba 6900
Tel: 2239-4598
Fax: 2259-2191
www.redeprotel.com.br
Beachfront. The Protel group manages a number of all-suite hotels, mainly in the Barra area. All have fully equipped kitchens, as well as complete hotel services. An excellent option if traveling with children. This sort of property is known as a Hotel Residência or Apart-Hotel. $

Flamengo
Flórida Hotel
Rua Ferreira Viana 81
Tel: 2555-6000
Fax: 2285-5777
www.windsorhoteis.com.br
Somewhat off the tourist track, but quite well located, just 10 minutes from Copacabana, and handy for the Metro. $

Hotel Novo Mundo
Praia do Flamengo 20
Tel: 2105-7000
Fax: 2265-2369
www.hotelnovomundo-rio.com.br
A Rio landmark, with spectacular views of Sugar Loaf Mountain. Graciously appointed accommodation at extremely attractive rates, but no pool. $

HEALTH AND EMERGENCIES

Hygiene/General Health
While Rio's tap water is technically safe to drink, it doesn't taste very good, due to high levels of chlorine; bottled water, which is easily available, is recommended instead.

An unwelcome visitor to Rio's summers

in recent years has been dengue fever. There are two kinds of dengue; one merely makes you feel ill all over, the other is far more dangerous. There is no prevention, but cases are, generally speaking, limited to the poorer, low-lying suburbs. If you think you may have dengue, seek medical advice, and under no circumstances take aspirin, as this can make things worse.

One much under-estimated cause of illness in the tropics is dehydration. Drink plenty of water, fruit juices, or coconut water; anything to keep your liquid levels up. Alcohol does not count – on the contrary, it has a dehydrating effect.

Pharmacies
Brazilians are great consumers of medication, and highly competitive pharmacies fight for custom on most main roads. All pharmacies are required to have a resident pharmacist on site; this can be helpful if you don't know what you need. 'Prescription-only' drugs are just that: prescription only.

Medical/Dental Services
Make sure your travel/health insurance covers you for all eventualities. Private out-patient treatment is excellent, but it is also costly. Private hospitals are very expensive, and you may be required to leave a sizeable (if illegal) deposit to guarantee payment, prior to admission. Call your consulate *(see page 91)* for names of doctors and dentists who speak your language.

Emergencies
The fire brigade operates an excellent trauma ambulance service, but they only transport people from the scene of an accident to a public hospital. For visitors, the most central public emergency unit is at Hospital Miguel Couto, Avenida Bartolomeu Mitre 1108, Gávea, tel: 2274-6050. Despite the apparent chaos, it is extremely well equipped.

Crime/Trouble
Rio's reputation for crime is, unfortunately, justified. Like any big city where rich and poor co-exist, petty thievery and pick-pocketing are prevalent. Be sensible, and carry nothing with you that you would miss too much if you lost it. Never, ever, react or

try to answer back if you are accosted in the street. Just do as you are told, and withdraw quietly. Also remember that dabbling in illegal drugs is a certain way to cut short your holiday.

Police
Rio's Tourist Police service has a special station for dealing with visitors, at Avenida Afrânio de Melo Franco 159, Leblon, tel: 3399-7171. If you are involved in an incident, it makes sense to report it, however inconvenient this may seem, as by doing so you may help prevent a fellow visitor suffering the same fate. You also need to report stolen property within 24 hours for your own insurance purposes.

Useful Numbers
Police: 190
Tourist Police: 3399-7171
Ambulance: 193
Fire Brigade: 193

COMMUNICATIONS AND MEDIA

The Brazilian postal service is reliable and up to international standards. Fax and internet facilities are available at many post offices and in some hotels.

Telephone
Cell phones can be rented from a number of companies, among them Press Cell. They will deliver your phone to you in Rio and you can return it anywhere in Brazil. They can tell you before you leave home what your number is going to be, which may be

Right: 'Big Ears', the public phones

useful if keeping in touch is important to you. Check them out on www.presscell.com.

Public phone booths, called *orelhões* (big ears) are hooded and blue, and take phone cards, which can be bought from newsstands.

Rio de Janeiro telephone numbers have eight digits. To call outside the Rio area, you need to dial one of the several different service providers (21, 31, or 23) plus the area code and then the number.

To make overseas calls, you dial 00 plus the service provider plus the country code plus the area code plus the number.

Local directory assistance: 102

Newspapers

Same-day editions of international newspapers are available, at a fairly high cost, from many newsstands in the city. For Rio newspapers with listings, see the 'What's On' section below.

WHAT'S ON?

Bilingual (English/Portuguese) listings of forthcoming events can be found in the Rio Tourist Authority's *RioGuide*, published six times a year. *Rio Show* is *O Globo*'s entertainment supplement; the *Jornal do Brasil*'s what-to-do guide is in *Programa*, both published on Friday. If you miss them, *Veja*, the weekly national news magazine, has a glossy insert called *Vejinha*, another what's-on guide, published on Sunday and available throughout the week. These last three are in Portuguese, but if used in conjunction with this book, they can provide understandable and useful information.

OUTDOOR ACTIVITIES

The art of entertaining foreign visitors comes naturally to the *cariocas*. Hundreds of individuals and organizations, small agencies as well as the full-service, mega-operators, offer a huge range of activities, adventures and unconventional ways to enjoy and view the city. Check with your hotel for their favored operators. The following is just a sample of what is available:

Lots of people want to **hang-glide**, either tandem or solo, when they get to Rio. Most flights land at the Praia do Pepino, the stretch of São Conrado beach furthest from Leblon. Operators stationed there will drive you up through the jungle to the take-off point on Pedra Bonita. Alternatively, you should contact the **Associação Brasileira de Vôo Livre**, tel: 3322-0266.

There are some truly magnificent options for **mountain climbing and hiking**, but many require expert guidance. Contact the **Centro Excursionista do Rio de Janeiro**, tel: 2220-3548, for a list of qualified guides.

Cycling is a great way to see the city, which is criss-crossed by cycle paths. English-speaking **Special Bike** will deliver a bike to your hotel from their office in Ipanema, at Rua Visconde de Pirajá 135, tel: 2521-2686; approximately US$12 per day.

Jungle Tours are popular. They take you deep into the Tijuca rainforest in especially equipped vehicles. **Indiana Jungle Tours**, tel: 2484-2279, offers a full service, with special emphasis on the environment.

Tropical Island Tours, tel: 2487-1687, cruise the Costa Verde islands, departing

from Itacuruça. These tours can be arranged through your hotel or local operators.

Favela Tours sound like the worst sort of voyeurism, but they are not: care is taken to show the positive side of community living in the shanties, and the residents are welcoming and proud of their achievements. The pioneer provider of these tours is Marcelo Armstrong, tel: 3322-2727.

Brazil Expedition, tel: 2513-4091, is another operator that specializes in tailoring **custom tours** for visitors with a taste for going off the beaten track .

Cruising and Boating: two reputable boat specialists that offer a full range of nautical options are: **Marlin Yacht Charters**, Marina Da Glória, shop No. A1, Glória, tel: 2225-7434; and **Saveiros Tours**, Rua Conde de Lajes 44/1001, Gloria, tel: 2224-6990 or 2252-1155.

THE GAY SCENE

Rio is a magnet for gay people, as they are warmly welcomed and accommodated. Check out the http://riogayguide.com website to see just how organized the city's gay community is. In newspaper or magazine listings, events and venues specifically catering to gay people are flagged GLS (Gays, Lesbians, and Sympathizers).

Left: taking flight at São Conrado
Above: Scala nightclub's Gay Ball

USEFUL ADDRESSES

Tourist Offices

The city's tourist authority, **Riotur**, has an office at Avenida Princesa Isabel 183, Copacabana, tel: 2541-7522. This is on the wide avenue that demarcates Copacabana from Leme. Riotur also runs a help line, **Alô Rio**, tel: 2542-8080 or 0800-707-1808, where multilingual operators will point you in the right direction.

Rio State's tourist authority, **Turisrio**, has offices in Centro at Rua Mexico 125, ground floor, tel: 2215-0001, and on the ground floor of Rio Sul shopping center in Botafogo (no phone). They have leaflets and assorted information about destinations outside the city limits, such as Búzios, Petrópolis and the Costa Verde.

Consulates

Most consulates close for lunch and many do not open at all in the afternoon, so do call ahead.
Argentina: Praia de Botafogo 228, Botafogo
Tel: 2553-1646.
Australia: Avenida Presidente Wilson 231, 23rd floor, Centro.
Tel: 2553-1646.
Canada: Avenida Atlântica 1130, 5th floor, Copacabana.
Tel: 2543-3004.
France: Avenida Presidente Antonio Carlos 58, 6th floor, Centro.
Tel: 2210-1272.
Germany: Rua Presidente Carlos de Campos 417, Laranjeiras.
Tel: 2553-6677.
Italy: Avenida Presidente Antonio Carlos 40, 7th floor, Centro.
Tel: 2282-1315 or 2220-3075.
Portugal: Avenida Marechal Câmara 160/1809, Centro.
Tel: 2544-2444.
South Africa: Rua David Campista 50, Botafogo.
Tel: 2527-1455.
UK: Praia do Flamengo 284, 2nd floor, Flamengo.
Tel: 2555-9600.
USA: Avenida Presidente Wilson 147, Centro
Tel: 2292-7117.

ACKNOWLEDGEMENTS

All Photography by	**Eric Carl Font** *except*
5, 76, 77, 78, 79, 91,	**Campos & Davis Photos/Apa**
10, 11, 12, 13	**Corbis**
14	**Mary Evans Picture Library**
16	**Rex Features**
15	**Vange Millet** *(courtesy of Aceno Galeria de Arte)*
Cover	**Frank Chmura/Alamy**
Back Cover	**Eric Carl Font** *(top)*
	Campos & Davis Photos/Apa *(bottom)*
Cartography	**Mapping Ideas Ltd**

© APA Publications GmbH & Co. Verlag KG Singapore Branch, Singapore

INDEX

index